DOPAMINE TRAP

Sexuality and Pornography in the 21st Century

PRASENJEET DHAGE

INDIA • SINGAPORE • MALAYSIA

Notion Press

No. 8, 3rd Cross Street,
CIT Colony, Mylapore,
Chennai, Tamil Nadu – 600 004

First Published by Notion Press 2020
Copyright © Prasenjeet Dhage 2020
All Rights Reserved.

ISBN 978-1-63606-677-6

*In the loving memory of my grandfather to
whom this book is dedicated
Pralhad
(May 11, 1946–September 15, 2016)
who taught me*
"The beginning of all knowledge is humility"

But 'tis strange

And oftentimes, to win us to our harm,

The instruments of darkness tell us truths…

– William Shakespeare,
Macbeth, Act I, scene iii

Contents

Acknowledgements

Many of the ideas in this book have engaged me for some time. When I first sat down to write this book, the creation began as a joyful yet solitary one; there was just the desktop and me. Then, gradually, the circle began to widen, encompassing more and more people, all of whom contributed their expertise before this book came in your hands.

I must say this book has been in many ways a collective effort. I am by all my heart truly thankful to my father Prabhakar Dhage who himself is an author of twelve books. He motivated me to write this book when I was a tad bit nervous and sceptical about the topic. My dear friend Saurabh S. Shirodkar who saw the writer in me four years ago and encouraged me to try my hand at writing, I am forever grateful to him. Apoorva Bandekar my friend who worked side by side with me on the cover of the book, I am thankful to her.

Prof. Dr. Ranjana Ferrão who kindled my interest in juvenile delinquency and whose knowledge and wisdom in the subject is vast; I am blessed to have her as my professor in Law College. Writer Mahaveer Jondhale his knowledge of sexuality in ancient India is impeccable. It is through conversations with him I could complete a chapter on sexuality. Artist Sunil

Yawlikar who gifted me his sketches inspired by the ideas of this book, he is too kind. I am grateful to Notionpress team especially Deepika Subhash the publishing manager. Getting the book into the market is definitely not an easy process. Thank you for being patient and working with me.

Finally, I would like to express my profound gratitude to you…the reader! There is nothing more rewarding than seeing that another copy of Dopamine Trap is getting sold. It is through a reader like you that an author like me grows and gets his encouragement to write more.

Introduction

People often wonder, is porn good for them? Is it liberating or is it confining? Is it empowering or is it addictive? Can we draw a line between Eroticism and perversion? What is moral and immoral in sexuality? This book tries to explore these questions and possibly find answers with empirical research.

Humankind has gone massive change concerning how we understand sex and sexuality. In ancient India, there were smritis which are basically codified laws these stated how a human should be and regulated the relationship between humans and between the state, smritis like the *manusmriti* had a profound understanding of sex it gives us an insight about how the Indians of 200 CE understood sex likewise the *Kamsutra* not only talks about various sex positions but also give us scientific knowledge as it was understood by the ancient Indians.

This book tries to explore how our understanding of sex has changed from generation to generation. The dawn of the internet has been responsible for the exponential rise of online pornography and how dopamine a neurotransmitter in the body reacts to it. The succeeding generations having online porn just a click away have explored all sorts of sexual desires, as the demand for each type of porn genre grew so did the supply for that is the fundamental law of economics which is also applicable to porn industry this has also changed the way how men and women look at relationships and have set different standards for body types, taste, sound, sex positions and longevity. In some cases, various sexual dysfunctions also have come into the light which is the direct by-products of porn.

Studies have shown that Porn can also change the structure of the brain and how dopamine and reward structure works which makes people want different and extreme types of porn more with continued usage. Essentially porn is subconsciously affecting all the areas of our life from a relationship with different people to criminality in society porn has changed our society just like media which is responsible to set trends and standards for fashion, food, lifestyle etc. porn has also subtly changed the old trends and standards since the dawn of the internet and this book makes an effort to explore these and the hazards that porn industry has brought with it. The debate on pornography in Western culture is broadly divided into two camps. The first being a sex-positive perspective which embraces the sexual revolution and sexual freedom. The second being the harm perspective, seeing pornography as exploitative, and harmful.

Pornography is not only just wanting to look at nude videos and pictures it has gone much beyond pleasure. It depends on how the chemicals in our brain react and how we perceive things. Our brain on porn is much more complicated than we think.

When I asked my friends about Porn many were okay with it. "It's a personal choice," they said, "neither good nor bad, neither right nor wrong". They were intrigued when I told them in some cases porn can have pernicious influences. Many of them believed that porn is liberating and sex-positive while others inferred that it could be addictive too. To me getting hooked to images and videos online seemed implausible.

Addiction is a compulsive need and use of the habit-forming substance.[1] This later develops into a brain disease that is manifested by compulsive substance use despite harmful consequences. Both compulsive substance use disorder and gambling are accompanied by anxiety and depression.[2]

Persons with a substance use disorder continue to pursue the activity despite it having detrimental effects. One drink leads to more drinks or one line of cocaine leads to more. Substance addiction makes people dependent, making it all the more difficult the quit, eventually this takes over their life. There is evidence that using these substances for a long period creates neurological changes which result in distorted thinking due to Changes in the brain's wiring. As a matter of fact, change in brain wiring is what causes people to have intense cravings for the drug and make it hard to stop using the drug. Similarly, some addictions like gambling can involve an inability to stop partaking in activities. These are known as behavioural addictions.

Drug and alcohol users' Brain imaging studies show changes in the areas of the brain that relate to judgment,

---

[1] Hesse, Morten. "What does addiction mean to me." Mens sana monographs vol. 4,1 (2006): 104-26. doi:10.4103/0973-1229.27609. Retrieved from https://www.ncbi.nlm.nih.gov/pmc/articles/PMC3190444/

[2] Physician Review By: Ranna Parekh, M.D., M.P.H, 'What Is Addiction?', *American Psychiatric Association,* January 2017. Retrieved from https://www.psychiatry.org/patients-families/addiction/what-is-addiction

decision making, learning, memory and behaviour control. The good thing about our brain is that it is capable of being rewired. But this needs time for healing, drugs like opioid have high levels of positive reinforcement hence they have lifelong negative consequences and are more difficult to quit than others. Substances like these can cause harmful changes in how the brain functions and these can last long after the immediate effects of the drug which is the intoxication. Intoxication can be defined as feelings of calm, intense pleasure, increased senses or a high caused by the drug. Intoxication symptoms are different for each substance.[3]

Over time, these drugs build up a tolerance and this means that they need to consume more and more drugs to get the same high. This is where the addiction takes over self-control.

According to the National Institute on Drug Abuse, people begin taking drugs for a variety of reasons, including:[4]

- to feel good—feeling of pleasure, "high"
- to feel better—e.g., relieve stress
- to do better—improve performance
- curiosity and peer pressure

Drug addiction impairs the ability of addicts to make sound decisions. According to the World Health Organisation, there are 275 million people who use illicit drugs and Some 31 million people who use drugs suffer from drug use disorders. While some countries have decriminalised marijuana, other hardcore drugs like cocaine, meth and opium are still illegal. But these drugs were not illegal 300 to 400 years back; in fact, there was an active trade of opium in China. Great Britain was buying large

---

[3]   Ibid.

[4]   Ibid.

quantities of tea from China but in return, they had very little to offer the Chinese.[5] This resulted in the drain of the wealth of Great Britain. Eventually, as they colonised India the steady drain of British silver to pay for the tea was stopped. The British merchants controlled much of India's trade and grew financially. Meanwhile, as the demand for tea in Great Britain increased they exported opium and cotton from India to China. Like any other psychoactive substance, opium was highly addictive. The increasing Chinese addiction fed a boom for opium exports. Opium deteriorated the Chinese addicts mentally as well as physically. The aim of British merchants was simple – to maximise profits, ironically they never sold huge quantities of opium in Britain for the sun sets on the British Empire but opium addiction would mean the sun would set forever.

Opium is produced from Opium Poppy. Drugs like Heroin come from the gum of opium poppies.[6] The production of this drug is quite labour intensive. The primary narcotic agent in opium is morphine. The morphine-rich sap of the poppy is derived from incisions made in the bulbous portion of the flower. United Nations Office on drugs and crime defines the effects of opium on the human body as, "sought-after effects" include a "sense of wellbeing by reducing tension, anxiety and depression; euphoria, in large doses warmth, contentment, relaxed detachment from emotional as well as physical distress" "Long-term effects" include, among a host of other things, "rapid development of tolerance and physical and psychological

---

5   Richard A. Webster, Charles E. Nowell and Harry Magdoff, 'Western colonialism' *Encyclopædia Britannica*, November 05, 2018. Retrieved from https://www.britannica.com/topic/Western-colonialism

6   Stephanie Pappas, 'Massive Poppy Bust: Why Home-Grown Opium Is Rare' *livescience.com*, June 12, 2017. Retrieved from https://www.livescience.com/59452-why-opium-is-grown-outside-us.html

dependence" and, in the case of "abrupt withdrawal," "moderate to severe withdrawal syndrome which is generally comparable to a bout of influenza (with cramps, diarrhoea, running nose, tremors, panic, chills and sweating, etc.).

In the 19th century, Britain fought with China over the right to trade opium with China. The British victory ensured that European powers would have continued access to the Chinese market for opium. The British East India Company employed Some 2,500 clerks working in 100 offices of a powerful colonial institution called the Opium Agency which monitored poppy farmers[7], enforced contracts and quality with police-like authority. Strict monitoring of the trade was required as opium trade would fetch major revenue for the British Crown. In the burgeoning international trade, exports of opium increased from 4,000 chests per year at the beginning of the 19th century to more than 60,000 chests per year by the end of 1880s! This was regarded as the second-most important source of revenue for the colonial state.

During world war I and world war II era too, drugs were easily available to injured soldiers many of the war veterans who fought in World War I had become addicted to these drugs. Addiction to drugs was thought to be assuredly curable.

It was Sun Tzu who wrote the Art of War who believed that speed is "the essence of war."[8] Well, he obviously didn't know about the performance-enhancing drugs which were used in the world wars and it is no surprise that Hitler's Nazi army

---

[7] Soutik Biswas, 'How Britain's opium trade impoverished Indians' *BBC News*, 5 September 2019. Retrieved from https://www.bbc.com/news/world-asia-india-49404024

[8] Peter Andreas, 'How Methamphetamine Became a Key Part of Nazi Military Strategy', *TIME*, January 7, 2020. Retrieved from https://time.com/5752114/nazi-military-drugs/

was named Blitzkrieg which signifies "The Lightening war" many powerful war-facilitating psychoactive drugs were used, Amphetamines also called as "pep pills," "go pills," "uppers" or "speed"—these are a group of synthetic drugs that stimulate the central nervous system, reducing fatigue and appetite and increasing wakefulness and a sense of well-being. While these drugs were used by Japanese, British and American forces the Nazi Germans were particularly very enthusiastic while using it. While most drugs were fundamentally thought to be a sign of personal weakness and the reason for the fall of the German Empire in the First World war, methamphetamine conflictingly although a drug was the privileged exception. Privileged because it was the perfect Nazi drug energizing and confidence-boosting something that was much needed for the Nazis to feel superior in intellect as well as in physical strength to dominate the world and establish Hitler's dream of 'Third Reich'. These drugs were taken not to escape reality but to have a hyper-awareness and vigilance for the Superior Aryans who were regarded by the Nazis as the perfect humans.

Methamphetamine also supported the idea of Hitler a.k.a the Nazi Führer who aspired to make superhumans and in turn these superhumans he could turn into super soldiers. As medical historian Peter Steinkamp puts it, "Blitzkrieg was guided by methamphetamine." "If not to say that Blitzkrieg was founded on methamphetamine." Between April and July 1940, German servicemen received more than 35 million methamphetamine tablets. The drug was even dispensed in the form of chocolate bars known as Fliegerschokolade (flyer's chocolate) which was distributed to pilots and Panzerschokolade (tanker's chocolate) for tank crew.[9] However towards the end of 1940 when many

---

[9] Ibid.

Nazi soldiers experienced side-effects like heart attacks and heart pains these performance-enhancing drugs saw their decline, as matter of fact they were also declared addictive and discontinued.

Theodor Morell, Führer's personal physician gave him medications for his intestine infection. Being Hitler's personal physician the duo grew a very close relationship that would last for more than nine years. During this time, Morell's notes show, the doctor injected Hitler almost daily with various drugs, including amphetamines, barbiturates and opiates.[10] Morell's personal notes suggest that he had given Hitler about eight hundred injections over the years; these injections were nothing but synthetic opiate oxycodone. He had also taken this drug before meeting Benito Mussolini in 1943 this was the time when things were not working out for the Axis powers. Later when Hitler committed suicide in 1945 along with his new wife Eva Braun in a bunker, he was likely suffering from withdrawal symptoms as Morell could not find the drugs in the destroyed city.

These days it is absolutely unimaginable to think about people using drugs on such an industrial level that too without prescription but these speed pills among other drugs were normalised in Nazi Germany.

Another type of drug used during World War II was morphine. Morphine is an alkaloid found in opium. Hermann Wilhelm Göring was appointed as the Reich Marshall and Airforce commander a high Ranking Nazi in Hitler's Germany, having suffered several injuries while taking part in a military

---

[10] Sarah Pruitt, 'Inside the Drug Use That Fueled Nazi Germany', *history. com*, July 18, 2019. Retrieved from https://www.history.com/news/ inside-the-drug-use-that-fueled-nazi-germany

coupe Herman was prescribed Morphine to ease his pain of bullet injuries. He soon got addicted to it.[11] Despite his exacting and ruthless rule, Göring had an erratic inner life as a morphine addict. His morphine addiction was so severe that he had to be institutionalized at a mental hospital in Sweden not once but twice in 1925 and 1926.

These days doctors use morphine in rare conditions owing to its addictive characteristics, even when used the doctors Before starting treatment with morphine, a discussion is held with patients to put in place a strategy for ending treatment with morphine to minimise the risk of addiction and drug withdrawal syndrome[12] and then it is gradually decreased so that there are no withdrawal symptoms.

However, this procedure was not followed strictly in the World War II era and morphine was readily available to Hermann who had gotten addicted to it because it gave him a euphoric feeling and the dopamine which ultimately increases the amount of pleasure felt. People with addictive disorders may be aware of their problem, but are unable to stop it even if they want to. So the question arises is how does substance addiction alter our brain to an extent that we lose control and become addicted to it?

Morphine causes Euphoria and Dreamlike experience also the Chemicals that interact with Morphine receptors on the nerve cells in the human body and brain and reduce feelings

---

[11] Joe Martin, "Book Review: 'Blitzed: Drugs in the Third Reich'", *Real Change News*, August 8th, 2018. Retrieved from https://www.realchangenews.org/2018/08/08/book-review-blitzed-drugs-third-reich

[12] 'Morphine Sulfate 10 mg/ml solution for injection', *medicines.org*, 1 April 2020. Retrieved from https://www.medicines.org.uk/

of pain.[13] After each usage, the addict needs more and more morphine to feel the Euphoria. Prolonged usage can cause depression or central nervous system overdose can cause death.

A morphine addict will get dependent on the drug because it messes up the Dopamine & reward system of the brain. Think of it like this each time you complete an assignment or complete a workout in the gym you feel good about it this is your brain's reward system working as you complete a task you get a rush of dopamine and your receptors in your brain reacts to it making you feel good. In Case of drugs like morphine the feedback mechanism in the brain which tells you if its meaningless pleasure or not is compromised and the user becomes an addict of the drugs even though it deteriorates the health and over some time the tolerance level for the drug increases and the user need higher doses which leads to overdose and death.

Some researchers say that Porn addiction is, in fact, possible but on the other side, pornography addiction is not directly defined in the latest edition of the Diagnostic and Statistical Manual of Mental Disorders, which doctors use to diagnose mental disorders. Moreover, there is an increasing trend among teenagers that pornography is liberating and unlike Speed pills; one doesn't consume porn via the mouth. Porn is just a visual that people use to satisfy their sexual pleasure. How did this pornography come into being?

---

[13] 'What Are the Mental and Physical Effects of a Morphine High?', *American Addiction Centres*, June 10, 2019. Retrieved from https:// americanaddictioncenters.org/morphine-treatment/mental-and-physical-effects

Porn Industry

According to various reports, the net worth of the porn industry is approximately 97 billion![14] From adult playboy magazines to online porn the industry has gone through rapid change in the last 50 years. Today even if there is 'hush-hush' around the world 'porn' almost every single person has watched it or come across it by accident. The beginning of society's most recent view of sexuality and porn can be partially attributed to Dr. Alfred Kinsey, the founder of the Kinsey Institute for Research in Sex, Gender, and Reproduction. Alfred Charles Kinsey was an American biologist, professor of entomology and zoology, and sexologist, Kinsey published his book, Sexual Behavior in the Human Female in 1953.[15]

He is best known for writing Sexual Behavior in the Human Male (1948) and Sexual Behavior in the Human Female (1953) At the time, some considered this to be part

---

[14] Strange But True, 'How Big is the Porn Industry?', *medium.com*, February 19, 2017. Retrieved from https://medium.com/@TheSBT/how-big-is-the-porn-industry-fbc1ac78091b

[15] 'The Evolution Of Porn: Where It Started, And How It Became So Normalized', *fightthenewdrug.org* January 25, 2017. Retrieved from https://fightthenewdrug.org/how-we-got-here-the-spread-of-porn/

of the most triumphant and significant scientific publications of the 20th century, stating that they proved that most people engaged in the sexual practices that society labelled as "taboo" and "deviant." However, when we dig deeper we understand the candour behind this. Kinseys' methodology in research involved collaborating with child molesters hence it has met with many criticisms. Before Kinsey, most physicians or psychologists did sex research on their patients; like Sigmund Freud who would write detailed narratives of people's sexual histories in his book although these research were fascinating it did not tell us if other people felt this way.[16] The experiments conducted by Kinsey on sexual behaviour were dubious, in the sense that, along with interviewing paedophiles, his research had a significant number of prisoners and male prostitutes.

Dr. Kinsey's controversial investigation went beyond research, he watched, motivated, and even filmed co-workers participating in sexual acts in the attic of his house. James H. Jones, whose "Alfred C. Kinsey: A Public/Private Life" appeared in 1997 mentions about the life of Dr. Kinsey.[17] Mr. Jone's book reveals that Dr. Kinsey had affairs with men moreover he also engaged in stimulating himself with urethral insertion and ropes. He was a twisted man who encouraged promiscuity, open marriages and even tried to circumcise himself. And what's more, Kinsey's documents have reported with over 300 children between the ages of five months and

---

[16] Rebecca A. Clay, 'Sex research at the Kinsey Institute. Psychologists have long played a major role at the Kinsey Institute. Here's what they are exploring now.' Vol 46, No. 9, *American Psychological Association.* October 2015. Retrieved from https://www.apa.org/monitor/2015/10/research-kinsey

[17] Caleb Crain, 'Alfred Kinsey: Liberator or Pervert?' *The News York Times,*October 3 2004. Retrieved from https://www.nytimes.com/2004/10/03/movies/alfred-kinsey-liberator-or-pervert.html

14 years old. The problem with his research was he sometimes interviewed sex criminals and failed to report their behaviour to police thereby risking public safety. It is no surprise that Judith Reisman, author of the 1990 book "Kinsey, Sex, and Fraud[18] led the anti-Kinsey movement who believed that Kinsey was responsible for the rising sexual crimes of all types.

Kinsey's research helped to normalize some of our society's misguided attitudes about sexuality and paved the way for the booming business of pornography. In December of 1953, the same year that Dr. Alfred Kinsey published Sexual Behavior in the Human Female in the same year the first issue of "Playboy," was published which featured early-career nude photos of Marilyn Monroe and sold over 50,000 copies[19]. Due to this Playboy became the world's most recognized porn brand. But did Dr. Kinsey's research lead to sexual liberation or perversion? Because the United States saw a 418% increase in reported forcible rape from 1960 to 1999, and that does not include children. And from 1960 to 1999, a 400% increase in out-of-wedlock births.[20] The Playboy porn magazine founded by Hugh Hefner had the stage set for his booming business by Dr. Kinsey's twisted research.

---

[18] Dina Spectoroct, 'Why Kinsey's Research Remains Even More Controversial Than The 'Masters Of Sex', *Business Insider, India.* October 18, 2013, Retrieved from https://www.businessinsider.in/ Why-Kinseys-Research-Remains-Even-More-Controversial-Than-The-Masters-Of-Sex160160160/articleshow/24345989.cms

[19] Ruth Umoh, 'How Hugh Hefner started with $600 and created the $110 million Playboy empire' September 28 2017. *CNBC, Make it.* Retrieved from https://www.cnbc.com/2017/09/28/hugh-hefner-used-600-to-start-the-110-million-playboy-empire.html#:~:text=In%20 1953%2C%20Hefner%20founded%20Playboy,she%20believed%20 in%20her%20son.%E2%80%9D

[20] EWTN, 'Kinsey's Flawed Research', EWTN. Retrieved from https:// www.ewtn.com/catholicism/library/kinseys-flawed-research-2719

Hefner maximised profits on the trend with his magazine. However, to increase more sales, he had to change porn's image; instead of being thought of it as something your friend's creepy uncle might have, porn had to be associated with "the man of honour" people would buy these magazines only if it looked like a gentleman's pursuit. To do that, Hefner put pornographic photos next to essays and articles written by respected authors. In Playboy, porn looked chic and sophisticated. No wonder the magazine's monthly circulation peaked at 7 million issues in 1971.

In recent years however the magazine's sale has gone down due to the availability of free online porn. In recent years pornography grew so much that 30% of all net traffic is generated by porn sites but before we get into the history of porn industries we need to see how different capitalists have convinced people to consume their products. The growth of the cigarette industry here is noteworthy because both the industries have used deceptive means to lure their consumers into consuming their product.

Within 150 years of Columbus's finding "strange leaves" in the New World, tobacco was being used around the globe. Its rapid spread and widespread acceptance characterise the addiction to the plant *Nicotina tobacum*. Only the mode of delivery has changed. In the 18th century, snuff held sway; the 19th century was the age of the cigar; the 20th century saw the rise of the manufactured cigarette and with it a greatly increased number of smokers. At the beginning of the 21st century about one-third of adults in the world, including increasing numbers of women, used tobacco. It was in the 20th Century when the world saw a rise in tobacco use in the form of cigarette smoking. This was also the era when people became more health-conscious about the side effects of smoking but well informed and educated consumers are not good consumers to these private companies! The tobacco companies faced the danger of going into losses and even bankruptcy. This meant they would not make any profits so what was the solution?

Before studies showed the toll on health that cigarettes have, the Cigarette companies hired doctors to promote smoking! Yes, you read that right. The companies started giving royalties to Doctors and Pharmacists to promote smoking! Look at this advertisement from 1930 in which a doctor is seen promoting cigarettes.

A 1930 Lucky Strike advertisement.
From the collection of Stanford Research
Into the Impact of Tobacco Advertising

The physician who is grinning from ear to ear gives reassurance to a class of worried society about the health consequences of smoking[21]. People have the utmost respect for physicians hence if they are making a claim, and then it must be but naturally true. American Tobacco, maker of Lucky Strikes was the first cigarette company to use physicians in their ads. In 1930, it published an ad claiming "20,679 Physicians say, *LUCKIES are less irritating*" to the throat. The pack of cigarettes which he holds in the advertisement for his trusting patient is larger than his head, implying that it is all the more important.[22] A carton of cigarettes was sent to physicians along with a note which asked the physicians "if Lucky Strikes were less irritating than other brands" the note also said that a lot of people had already said the cigarettes were, in fact, less irritating than the rest. The results? Doctors responded in affirmative and that's how this advertisement came into being.[23]

Due to heavy Cigarette smoking, there was a spike in cases of cancer in the 1940s but people didn't stop or reduce smoking because they had no idea what gave them cancer. Yes, cigarettes did cause throat irritation and cough but this fuelled competition among the various brands who claimed that their cigarettes were "toasted" or had a "revolutionary filter" which made their cigarettes less irritating than others.

---

[21] From the collection of Stanford Research Into the Impact of Tobacco Advertising, Retrieved from http://tobacco.stanford.edu/tobacco_main/images.php?token2=fm_st002.php&token1=fm_img0101.php&theme_file=fm_mt001.php&theme_name=Doctors%20Smoking&subtheme_name=20,679%20Physicians

[22] Ibid

[23] Becky Little, 'When Cigarette Companies Used Doctors to Push Smoking', history.com, September 11, 2019. Retrieved from https://www.history.com/news/cigarette-ads-doctors-smoking-endorsement

The false health claims, like less irritating and throat protection against irritation against cough are utilized for years after the 20,679 campaign ends. Later, such health claims were alluded to solely by the slogan "It is toasted," which became a synonym for healthy. Even Doctors were seen smoking and offering cigarettes to patients who came to visit them on account of being ill.

Here is another advertisement in which the customers are informed where they can find their favourite cigarettes:

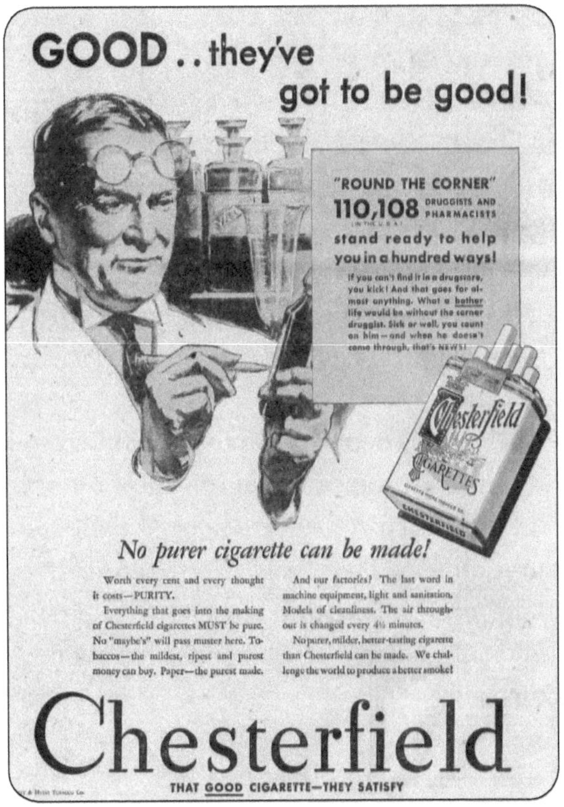

A 1931 Chesterfield advertisement.
From the collection of Stanford Research Into the Impact of
Tobacco Advertising

While promoting cigarettes even pharmacists were not left alone. This advertisement allows readers to know exactly where they can purchase Chesterfields from the local chemist & druggist. Pharmacists are presented in a similar light as doctors, as someone you can count on or trust.[24]

To suppress the consumers' fear about tobacco products one common technique adopted by the tobacco industry to reassure a worried public was to incorporate images of physicians in their ads. Tobacco companies used doctors in the advertisement to show that their brands were safe. There was paradox among these brands as one company ad would claim that their cigarette was not harmful in another ad of the same company they'd claim their cigarette was less harmful than others but unlike celebrity and athlete endorsers, the doctors depicted in these advertisements were never specific individuals, that is to say, this was merely a sketch or poster for the purpose of advertising. If real physicians were engaged in these advertising they would risk losing their license as a medical practitioner.

Such deception is deployed on the consumers to lure them into buying their unhealthy product which deteriorates their health and once the customers are hooked there is no turning back because out of 100% only 40% customers completely stop smoking ever which brings us to the question why is cigarette smoking so addictive? Now let's look at how smoking can be addictive:

---

[24] Ibid

Nicotine is the chemical in tobacco that keeps you smoking. An average cigarette has about 10 to 12 mg of nicotine[25] and a cigar will have 100 mg of nicotine. Nicotine gets into the body through cigarettes, activating structures normally present in your brain called receptors. These receptors are found in the central and peripheral nervous system, muscle, and many other tissues of many organisms.

When these receptors are activated, they release a brain chemical called dopamine, which makes you feel good. This pleasure response to dopamine is a big part of the nicotine addiction process. Let us understand what dopamine is Dopamine appeared very early in the course of evolution and is involved in many functions that are essential for the survival of the organism, such as mortality, attentiveness, motivation, learning, and memorization. But most of all, dopamine is a key element in identifying natural rewards for the organism. These natural stimuli such as food and water cause individuals to engage in approach behaviours. Dopamine is also involved in unconscious memorization of signs associated with these rewards.

It has now been established that all substances (including cigarettes) that trigger dependencies in human beings increase the release of a neuromodulator, dopamine, in a specific area of the brain.

Most people think smoking only affects their lungs and heart but we now know how smoking a cigarette influences dopamine. Over time, the number of nicotine receptors in your brain increases as one continues to smoke. Addicted smokers

---

[25] Tim Jewell, 'How Much Nicotine Is in a Cigarette and Other Tobacco Products?' November 18, 2019, *healthline*. Retrieved from https://www.healthline.com/health/how-much-nicotine-is-in-a-cigarette#:~:text=On%20the%20low%20end%2C%20a,to%20 12%20mg%20of%20nicotine.

have billions more of these receptors than non-smokers do. But not all smokers have such a high level of receptors. That is why some regular smokers can stop smoking without much difficulty. When you try to stop smoking, the receptors in your brain do not receive nicotine, so the pleasure response is cut off. Besides, low levels of nicotine lead to symptoms of nicotine withdrawal, such as strong cravings for a cigarette, anxiety, irritability, restlessness, difficulty concentrating, depressed mood, frustration, anger, increased hunger and difficulty sleeping. The fastest way to alleviate the withdrawal symptoms is to smoke a cigarette, which releases dopamine and activates the pleasure response.[26]

According to the National Institutes of Health, the nicotine in cigarettes changes your brain, which leads to withdrawal symptoms when you try to quit. This makes matters worse as the brain is conditioned in a way to expect more nicotine and when it is not provided withdrawal symptoms start appearing. For example, if you regularly smoke when you drink alcohol, or when you are in a stressful situation, or after a meal, the nicotine receptors in your brain anticipate the dopamine rush from nicotine at that time. These "trigger" situations can cause intense cravings for a cigarette, even if you have stopped smoking for several months.

Because of its effects on your brain, nicotine can be powerfully addictive this is why people find quitting difficult. For people, who are chain-smokers overcoming nicotine addiction and successfully dealing with its withdrawal symptoms requires medical treatment.

---

[26] Shawn Bishop, 'Smokers' Brains Change in Response to High Levels of Nicotine', *Mayo Clinic, News network*, February 24, 2012. Retrieved from https://newsnetwork.mayoclinic.org/discussion/smokers-brains-change-in-response-to-high-levels-of-nicotine/

The Dopamine

Various neurotransmitters and hormones are at work when a person watches porn but the most important one is dopamine, which plays a major role in how we feel pleasure. It's a unique evolutionary system which aids us to think and plan. Dopamine is the chemical located in the brain closely responsible for the emotions and actions[27]. It is the reward that your brain releases each time you complete a task. This evolutionary chemical is released in your brain to encourage you to learn more about something. It is also responsible for Motivation, Mood, Attention, Control of nausea and vomiting, Pain processing and Movement.

Every time we do something, whether it is answering a test, playing a sport, completing assignments, cleaning your room watching TV, eating food, etc., our brains release chemicals that dictate how we feel towards that specific action. Our brains then categorize these events as good or bad based upon what chemical is released. When something tastes good or feels

---

[27] Jacob Beck, 'How Pornography Affects Your Brain [is porn good for you?]', *everACCOUNTABLE*. Retrieved from https://everaccountable. com/blog/how-pornography-affects-your-brain/

good, dopamine is released which encourages us to seek that action again. This can also be called natural reinforcement.

The work of natural reinforcement is pretty straightforward. When we have a good meal, our body produces a moderate amount of dopamine, but when we have a great meal; our body releases an incredible amount of dopamine. I for once always enjoy a good dessert after lunch and dinner. Just like sex and dopamine, sugar and dopamine are heavily linked to each other each time you eat sugary food your brain gives a dopamine spike an extremely good dessert with a lot of sugar would give me even more dopamine spikes hence, it gives me a feeling of excitement and satisfaction but here's the deal… The presence of high amounts of dopamine, the brain removes dopamine receptors for balance. But, with fewer receptors, more dopamine is required to reach them. This is known as "tolerance," and is a tell-tale sign of addiction. Fewer dopamine receptors and less dopamine activity lead to feelings of unhappiness and the need to get a "fix." This is known as "withdrawal," another hallmark of addiction. So, naturally, you will want the incredible snack over the good snack. Too much or too little of dopamine can lead to a vast number of health issues.

Think about it, diets aside, would you rather eat an apple or a fudge brownie with a huge scoop of ice cream? I personally prefer the latter. Sweet-tooth might invite trouble and regular visits to the doctor but I read somewhere that an apple a day keeps anyone away if you throw it hard enough. Anyway, in addition to eating desserts, processed food and junk food can also cause serious psychological effects. Consumption of these foods causes the brain to release dopamine. When done repeatedly and chronically, the dopamine receptors will start to down-regulate.

It should be pretty apparent then, that dopamine plays a huge role in our decisions. Especially those things that give us immediate satisfaction.[28] We quintessentially only think that dopamine is behind our learned behaviours and not something that is actively aiding in decisions. Do you think humans are capable of taking decisions for themselves and you can predict their future decisions? In the March 9, 2017, online publication of the journal Neuron, scientists at the Salk Institute report that the concentration of a brain chemical called dopamine governs decisions about actions so precisely that measuring the level right before a decision allows researchers to accurately predict the outcome. Additionally, the scientists found that changing the dopamine level is sufficient to alter upcoming choices.[29] There is noteworthy research on rats which provides us with ample information on how people get addicted to porn due to dopamine.

The Salk Institute performed a study[30] which investigates the effects of dopamine on the decisions of mice. The study tracked mice as they made decisions requiring triggering two different levers to get a reward based upon how long the levers had disappeared for. If the triggers disappeared for 2 seconds the mice were rewarded for pushing the left trigger and at 8 seconds they received a reward from the right trigger.

The results? The mice were quick to learn to switch sides to get the treat. The scientists used real-time brain-scan, by the

---

[28] Ibid.

[29] Salk Institute, 'Hard choices? Ask your brain's dopamine', *medicalxpress,* March 9, 2017. Retrieved from https://medicalxpress.com/news/2017-03-hard-choices-brain-dopamine.html#jCp

[30] Ibid.

reason of which they were able to discern that the mice were making the decisions in correlation to the dopamine release. This suggests that dopamine is involved in on-going decisions as opposed to the initial learning process.

Christopher Howard a Salk research collaborator who is the paper's first co-author says, "We are very excited by these findings because they indicate that dopamine could also be involved in the on-going decision, beyond its well-known role in learning"

To verify these dopamine levels, scientists at Salk used some brain-altering devices to change the level of dopamine in real-time to try and cause the mice to make a different decision than they normally would. They found that they could force the mice to go whichever direction they wanted to by simply altering the amount of dopamine in their brains!

Humans have substantially more levels of dopamine all thanks to evolution.[31] This dopamine is one of the reasons why we as humans have developed into Homo-sapiens, from being hunter-gatherers and moving from place to place to developing cooperation over time with each other and building gigantic civilizations across the globe. It was Aristotle who said, human beings are "social animals" and therefore naturally seek the companionship of others as part of their wellbeing. Human beings cannot only procreate but also bond with mates, communicate through language, make tools, machines and make small talk with strangers on a packed bus. Put primates like monkeys in the same spot and most

---

[31] David Nield, 'This Could Be The One Key Hormone That Set Us Apart From Apes', *Sciencealert*, 27 January 2018. Retrieved from https://www.sciencealert.com/key-hormone-dopamine-could-set-us-apart-from-apes#:~:text=While%20it's%20found%20in%20both,leg%20up%20in%20evolutionary%20history.

wouldn't make it off the bus in one piece (pun intended). A new study suggests that the evolution of our unique social intelligence may have initially begun as a simple matter of brain chemistry.

Primates are distinguished for having hands, feet, forward-facing eyes that are similar to humans. Neuroanatomists who study the anatomy of organisms have been trying for years to find significant variances between the brains of humans and other primates, aside from the obvious brain size. The human brain saw its chemistry and wiring as early human ancestors began to walk upright, use tools, and develop more complex social networks 6 million to 2 million years ago. Compared with other primates, both humans and great apes had elevated levels of serotonin. However, as claimed by another recent study on gene expression, humans had dramatically more dopamine in their brain as compared to apes.[32] It's perhaps this chemical mix that has given us a trump card in evolutionary history.

The dopamine expansion in the early development period of Hominids has enabled them for successful hunting and gathering. Dopamines along with changed dietary habits help the brain size to increase; this made remarkable progress in human intelligence. The idea that dopamine is actually facilitating decision-making helps explain what happens during addiction or when we choose behaviours which counteract our beliefs, especially at the risk of negative feelings (guilt, shame, etc.).

---

[32] Ann Gibbons, 'dopamine may have given humans our social edge over other apes', *ScienceMag.org,* January. 22, 2018. Retrieved from https://www.sciencemag.org/news/2018/01/dopamine-may-have-given-humans-our-social-edge-over-other-apes.

When a user watches porn over some time the brain builds tolerance for the high levels dopamine that is secreted in the brain hence the same images and videos don't give the rush, to get more rush you need to watch more videos and more brutal hardcore porn. The case is the same with Heroin and cocaine even if the addicted user knows that it is wrong the thought is overridden by the constant need to satisfy the dopamine high.

Our brain is hardwired to seek out behaviours that release dopamine in the reward system. The craving for dopamine is so strong that it can overcome our body's defence mechanisms against performing unrewarding behaviours. This is why when you have an apple you will feel a small dopamine release while junk food like a good ol' cheeseburger will give you a lot of dopamine release. Hence frequent consumption of junk food[33] or in some cases even processed food can lead to tolerance. This is why many men and women chronically addicted to pornography will continue to watch it even though they know that is wrong or why a drug addict will continue to use even at the expense of their own health.

We have an affinity to want "new" things because they produce more dopamine–more excitement–and with pornography the options for new people is endless. John Mayer a renowned music artist actually commented on this, saying:

"There have probably been days when I saw 300 [women] before I got out of bed. Internet pornography has absolutely changed my generation's expectations. You're looking for the one photo out of 100 you swear is going to be the one you finish to, and you still don't finish. Twenty seconds ago you

---

[33] Kris Gunnars,'How Food Addiction Works (and What to Do About It)', *healthline,* December 4, 2019. Retrieved from, https://www. healthline.com/nutrition/how-food-addiction-works#tolerance-&-withdrawal

thought that photo was the hottest thing you ever saw, but you throw it back"[34]

The frequent consumption of porn also dulls the rewards function of the brain as addicts become lethargic and unmotivated to do anything. Watching porn could shrink a part of the brain linked to pleasure, according to a study from 2014. Researchers at the Max Planck Institute in Berlin looked at the brains of more than 60 men while they looked at pornographic images, and quizzed them on their porn-watching habits.[35]

The research findings concluded that the striatum, a critical part of the brain which constitutes the motor as well as a reward system, was smaller in those who had a higher pornography usage[36]. This meant that these consumers might require more graphic material to get aroused. Consequently, these striatums also show a change in size with addiction related to cocaine. But the researchers couldn't conclude if respondents with smaller striatums were driven to watch more porn, or if their frequent porn-watching had caused it to shrink – although they "assume" the latter is the case.

---

[34] Scott M Crocker, 'Crocker Chronicle, Thoughts on the intersection of race, religion, politics, ministry, sports and culture.', *crockerchronicle, blogspot.com*, Friday, April 30, 2010. Retrieved from http://crockerchronicle.blogspot.com/2010/04/john-mayer-on-porn-and-relationships.html

[35] Jessica Brown, 'Is porn harmful? The evidence, the myths and the unknowns', *BBC*, 26th September 2017. Retrieved from, https://www.bbc.com/future/article/20170926-is-porn-harmful-the-evidence-the-myths-and-the-unknowns

[36] Kühn S, Gallinat J, 'Brain Structure and Functional Connectivity Associated With Pornography Consumption: The Brain on Porn', *JAMA Psychiatry*, 2014, Retrieved from https://jamanetwork.com/journals/jamapsychiatry/fullarticle/1874574

In another research conducted by German Simone Kühn, a psychologist, and Jürgen Gallinat, a psychiatrist.[37] Wherein they scanned the brains of "64 healthy men and the researchers found that hours spent watching porn were "negatively correlated with the amount of grey matter in a subcortical region near the front of the brain – the right striatum – that's known to be involved in the processing of reward (as well as lots of other things)." These study subjects – who watched porn often had smaller striatum, which is an important part of the reward system and also involved in libido.[38] vis-a-vis, men who said they spent more time watching porn had more probability to have a smaller amount of grey matter in this part of their brain.

Of all the desires that the internet fuels, the desire for synthetic sex is, seemingly, by far the most lucrative, sought after, and abused desire of all.

Can we say that right now pornography, unfortunately, is the king of the internet?

One of the most unfortunate by-products of internet pornography is its crippling effects on men and women.

There are literally thousands of people who struggle with quitting watching porn, once it takes over their lives. More alarmingly, porn is actually changing consumers' brains and bodies for the worse.

---

[37] Tian Jarrett, 'Is It Really True That Watching Porn Will Shrink Your Brain?', *WIRED* June.19.2014. Retrieved from https://www.wired.com/2014/06/is-it-really-true-that-watching-porn-will-shrink-your-brain/

[38] Brigitte Osterath, 'Pea brain: watching porn online will wear out your brain and make it shrivel' *DW.org*, 05.06.2014. Retrived from https://www.dw.com/en/pea-brain-watching-porn-online-will-wear-out-your-brain-and-make-it-shrivel/a-17681654

Our mothers and fathers never had to deal with high-speed internet and easy access to porn. Porn has never even been as hardcore as it is today.

Let's look at how this new 21st-century pornography came into existence.

The Rise of the Internet

Internet, the world's most popular computer network. Today it is used by more than 2 billion people. Even though it is used by all countries the internet is surprisingly not owned by anyone instead, thousands of organizations operate on the internet and negotiate interconnection agreements. The internet basically started off as a U.S. Department of Defence funded project to communicate with different computers in the same network; however, it became a global commercial network only after the 1990s.

The explosion of pornographic content on the internet is noteworthy. In June 1995 inside the Senate chamber in Washington, D.C., and Jim Exon, a 74-year-old Democrat from Nebraska had begun his address to his colleagues He was there to urge his fellow senators to pass his and Indiana senator Dan Coats' amendment to the Communications Decency Act[39]. The amendment to this act would extend the

---

[39] David Kushner 'A Brief History of Porn on the Internet Pornographers developed many early innovations in internet marketing, like pop-up ads and subscriptions. And women were among the most successful entrepreneurs in the business' *WIRED*, 04.09.2019. Retrieved from https://www.wired.com/story/brief-history-porn-internet/

anti-decency laws to the world of the internet in the United States. The Democrat wanted "The minds of our children and the future and moral strength of our Nation to be saved from the indecent images available on the internet", little did he know how pervasive and ever-expanding these images would become in the coming 21st century. Exon warned that the websites were filled with the sort of "perverted pornography" that was "just a few clicks away". The study that he had conducted found that more than 450,000 pornographic images online that had been accessed by people approximately 6.4 million times in the previous year. The main source had been the free newsgroups sex, bestiality—and so on. The senators felt that this was a very delicate situation but even back then the concerns over such Pornographic websites were not new as adult magazines and porn VCR were very common.

Mankind is not new to Erotic Technological Impulse. 27,000 years ago among the first clay-fired figures uncovered from that time were women with large breasts and behinds. From the stone age to the Internet, sexual imagery has been common. When Sumerians, the indigenous people of ancient Babylonia discovered the art of writing on clay tablets some four thousand years ago, they filled it with sexual imagery.[40] There have been female nudes on walls of the La Magdelaine caves from 15,000 BC. One of the first films shown commercially was The Kiss in 1900, distributed by Thomas Edison, which depicted 18 seconds of a couple nuzzling.

---

[40] Ilan Ben Zion '4,000-year-old erotica depicts a strikingly racy ancient sexuality Clay plaques at The Israel Museum, made 1,500 years before the Kama Sutra, display graphically that Old Babylonian culture held an 'exalted' view of sex', *The Times of Israel,* 17 January 2014. Retrieved from https://www.timesofisrael.com/4000-year-old-erotica-depicts-a-strikingly-racy-ancient-sexuality/

The Time Magazine predicted the bane of porn back on July 3, 1995, just in time for holiday readers. The cover photo showed a young boy at a computer keyboard, bathed in blue light, eyes wide, mouth opened in horror. "CYBERPORN," the cover line screamed, "a new study shows how pervasive and wild it really is. Can we protect our kids—and free speech?" However, despite the federal regulation to prevent indecent images from surfacing online, there was simply no way to stop the flood of porn online, let alone determine or enforce the age of consumers. And now more people than ever were online.

As the Bourgeosing Porn industry grew in the United States, the federal government conveniently got out of their way. On June 26, 1997, after more than a year of heated debate about the censoring of the internet, the United States Supreme Court struck down the Communications Decency Act for violating the First Amendment. It was a landmark decision, protecting the young medium from government regulation.

In an online survey when we asked (mostly youth) if their close friends consume porn, 70% gave an affirmative answer. Porn itself isn't bad. Let's begin by saying a lot of people watch, read or listen to porn.

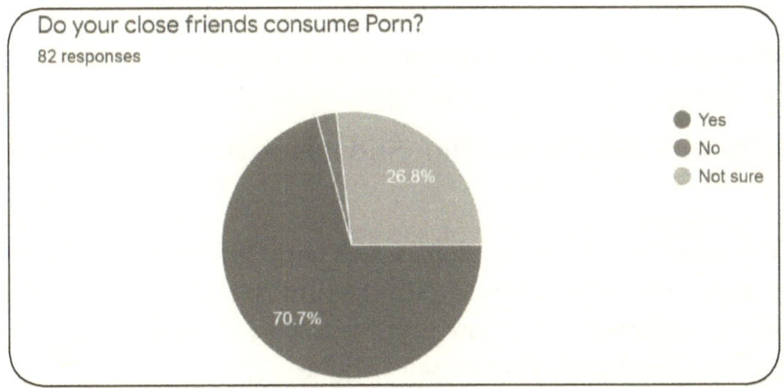

We live in a culture where we have an abundance of online content available on our smartphones, Hence access to billions of websites 24/7. Those days when people bought adult material only on at sex shops and shady book stores are long gone. Men and women both consume porn, some women find empowerment through it. The author of the book Rethinking Pornography, Richa Kaul Padte thinks "Many women, including myself, have found pornography to be a liberating space – especially because it facilitates pleasure that you can access on your own, and don't need a partner for."[41]

Today, when it comes to sexuality people, are oftentimes intimidated to explore and wonder sometimes if such things are normal. Nadika Nadja, a writer believes "Porn is an outlet for those who have been stigmatised in the society for their choices. It gives you pleasure and gratification, all at once."

In anthropological terms, if there is one thing that separates humans from animals is "privacy". Right to privacy is enshrined in article 12 of the Universal Declaration of Human Rights. Unlike animals, sex in public is so outrageous that it is even illegal.[42] Animals often learn behaviours by watching other animals, thankfully we don't have to stare at others to learn about sex. Advancement of technology means almost everything can be learnt on the internet if not it can be shown in pictures or video format. Concerning this, we share similarities with apes. A female gorilla born in a zoo can learn how to breastfeed its young through videos shown of other gorillas who did it in the wild. And it is no surprise that modern

---

[41] Priyanka Richi, 'Why do people watch porn? Five women explain their reasons' *The NEWS Minute,* NOVEMBER 09, 2018. Retrieved from https://www.thenewsminute.com/article/why-do-people-watch-porn-five-women-explain-their-reasons-91284

[42] Florence Walker, 'Why pornography is good for you', *GQ Mgazine,* 29 September 2015. Retrieved from https://www.gq-magazine.co.uk/article/why-porn-is-good-for-you

mothers often complain that breastfeeding is not instinctual. This could be because breastfeeding is not a common sight nowadays. Sex is no different than this hence we had sex manuals like *Kamasutra* in India and *Shunga-Shunga* in Japan to help people understand sex better.[43]

Humans don't have sex to merely procreate, as a matter of fact, psychologists argue that sex is a strategy we use to meet our psychological needs.

---

[43] Ibid

Evolution of Sex and Porn Industry

Approximately three million years ago a skeleton named 'Lucy' (nicknamed after the Beatles song: Lucy in the sky with diamonds) was found in Africa. She walked on two legs. Big deal you say!? Even toddlers know to walk! Well, you are not wrong but at least such records show that early humans did learn to walk the earth.[44] Her brain weighed merely 400 cc while modern humans have a brain of around 1,550 cc. Archaeologists have found some evidence that a family of nine such hominids (like Lucy) were killed in a sudden disaster – maybe their pea brains did not have dopamine reward structure mechanisms which would have motivated them to run, who knows?

Whether it's hominids, homo sapiens, vertebrate, non-vertebrate or other living beings they all have one characteristic in common--to make sure their species don't go extinct. This they could do via reproduction but all sexual activities do not lead to reproduction. Research has shown that Humans as well as animals engage in sex for different reasons.

---

[44] Pg.7, Terry Deary illustrated by MartinBrown, 'Stone Age timeline', *Horrible Histories Savge Stone Age.*

Earlier it was believed that animals engage in coitus for procreation only and that animals' sexuality was instinctive and a simple response to the "right" stimulation that is to say sight and scent. But now we have come to an understanding that many species engage in masturbation and use various tools to facilitate it, moreover the belief that animals have sex to reproduce is obsolete as many species don't adhere to monogamous relationships and are inclined to promiscuity. What's more, homosexual behaviour is not only observed among humans but 1500 recorded species on earth show homosexual behaviour. Our horizon of sexuality is ever-expanding as there is no end to scientific research.

Why do you think humans have sex? My ancestors i.e. homo sapiens and probably yours too who walked the earth 200,000 years ago did a lot of crazy experiments with sexuality. Even though their brains were not as developed as ours they had a knack for curiosity. Homosapiens had sex with Neanderthals, Denisovans, in fact, there are records of ancient humans having sex with gorillas! Yes, you read that right looks like we had a lot of choices to mate back in good ole' days.

Before the evolution of all organisms, reproduction occurred asexually. This means organisms literally split themselves in half to form 2 individual organisms. This type of reproduction was much more efficient than sexual reproduction this is because asexual species do not have to waste time and energy searching for and impressing a partner, they just grow and divide in two.[45] But these organisms evolved as sex had its own advantages. Sex allowed two different organisms to pool their resources

---

[45] Vivien Cumming, 'The Real Reason Why We Have Sex, What is the real story of the birds and the bees?', *BBC earth*, 4 July 2016. Retrieved from http://www.bbc.com/earth/story/20160704-the-real-reasons-why-we-have-sex

this essentially means the best genes from both the organisms got passed to their progeny. This will, in turn, help the new organisms to respond in a better way to the environment as compared to organisms who are reproduced asexually.

Science says that sex is a pleasurable experience for all humans. Human beings are inclined to sex because sex and procreation guarantee the continuity of genes. Reproduction helps in mutation and stronger offspring and bad DNA is overwritten. Scientists say a lot is going on in the body that makes sex feel good. These feelings of pleasure belong to a series of physical and emotional stages that you experience when you're having sex or feeling aroused. The brain is its own pleasure centre during coitus. Remember that time you were on a date with your partner and just being physically close with them gave you a warm feeling and happiness? This happens because of an increase in the levels of oxytocin—the "cuddle hormone"—in the brain, making you feel happy and secured.[46]

From pleasure to procreation, insecurity to inquisitiveness – today's reasons for having sex has many reasons.[47] Historically humans have had sex to make babies, to feel good, or because you're in love. Human beings are infinitely complex. Just as there is no universal reason for eating chips (whether trying to win a contest or eating them while binge-watching a Netflix

---

[46] Erica Cirin, 'Why Does Sex Feel Good?' *healthline*, October 10 2019. Retrieved from https://www.healthline.com/health/why-does-sex-feel-good#6

[47] Kelli Miller, 'The Top 20 Reasons People Have Sex Sexual motives go far beyond the 'Big Three' – love, pleasure, and making babies.', *WebMD*. Retrieved from https://www.webmd.com/sex-relationships/guide/why-people-have-sex#1

series, out of habit), there is no single reason in modern times which would explain why people engage in sex.

Porn on the other hand is quite different even though many humans want to imitate what they see in pornography. One porn star, Franziska describes real-life sex as more "flowing" because you don't have to stop to worry about how things look on camera. Lily Ivy says "you stop a lot during porn sex."

The upper house of parliament, The House of Lords, U.K. tried to define the word pornography in a government consultation paper published in 2005 as "the material which is explicit and has been solely, or primarily produced for the purpose of sexual arousal."[48] Whereas The word *pornography* is Defined in encyclopaedia Britannica, as being derived from the Greek *porni* ("prostitute") and *graphein* ("to write"), was originally defined as any work of art or literature depicting the life of prostitutes.[49]

History of pornography is nearly impossible to conceive; imagery that might be considered erotic or even religious in one society may be condemned as pornographic in another.

Sex and sexuality in ancient India were looked upon as a science to study for men and women who were reaching their adulthood. Modern India is one of the oldest civilizations in the world. Excavations in the Indus Valley trace civilization there back for at least 5,000 years. India's cultural history includes prehistoric mountain cave paintings in Ajanta, the exquisite beauty of the Taj Mahal in Agra, the rare sensitivity and warm emotions of the erotic Hindu temple sculptures

---

[48] Mary Santo, 'Impact of Pornography on Society', *House of Lords Library*, October 30, 2015. Retrieved from https://lordslibrary.parliament.uk/research-briefings/lln-2015-0041/

[49] John Philip Jenkins, "Pornography", *Brirannica.* Retrieved from https://www.britannica.com/topic/pornography

of the 9th-century Chandella rulers, and the Kutab Minar in Delhi. The seeming contradictions of Indian attitudes towards sex can be best explained through the context of history. India played a significant role in the history of sex, we can find the first literature that treated sexual intercourse as a science.

Nudity in art was considered acceptable in southern India, as shown by the paintings at Ajanta and the sculptures of the time. It is likely that as in most countries with tropical climates, Indians from some regions did not feel the need to wear full clothes, and other than for fashion, there was no practical need to cover the upper half of the body. This is supported by historical evidence, which shows that men in many parts of ancient India mostly dressed only the lower half of their bodies with clothes and upper part of the body was covered by gold and precious stones, jewellery, while women used to wear traditional sarees made of silk and expensive clothes as a symbol of their wealth. In another part of Kerala, a caste system prevalent 300 years ago, lower caste women were forbidden from covering their breasts.[50]

Vatsyayana's classic work "Kama-sutra" (Aphorisms of love) written somewhere between the 1st and 6th centuries includes the three pillars of the Hindu religion "Dharma," "Artha" and "Kama" representing religious duty, worldly welfare and sensual aspects of life respectively. The main theme here appears to be the expression of Indian attitude toward sex as a central and natural component of Indian psyche and life. While clothing style differed from place to place, people mainly wore clothes

---

[50] 'The woman who cut off her breasts to protest a tax' *BBC News,* 28 July 2016. Retrieved from https://www.bbc.com/news/world-asia-india-36891356

made of locally grown cotton. As early as 2500 B.C. there were cotton cultivations in Indus Valley civilization

Kamasutra was not all about sex positions it was to educate men and women about sex. The Kamasutra reveals relatively liberal attitudes to women's education and sexual freedom[51], for instance, the authors of the Kamasutra warn, "Women are like flowers, and need to be enticed very tenderly. If they are taken by force by men who have not yet won their trust they become women who hate sex". An elegant Subhashitha from Vishnusharma's Panchatantra clearly indicates the necessity of appropriate and adequate food/nutrition, a requisite for having the right mindset and power for optimum sexual performance. During the 10th century to the 12th century, some of India's most famous ancient works of art were produced, often freely depicting romantic themes and situations. Hence we can see that in ancient India sex was not looked upon as a taboo topic but a part of adult life which the indigenous people needed to have scientific knowledge of.

The Indian Goddess Kali Ma representing feminine energy, creativity and fertility is supposed to be the literally "better half" of Shiva. She is represented like a hermit semi-nude with cut hands around her waist as a skirt which represents karma and a garland of severed heads around her neck which symbolizes the repository of knowledge and wisdom and a severed head in her hand which represents the destruction of ignorance and the beginning of knowledge. Kali is basically Kal or time in female form, she is raw, devoid of people's

---

[51] 'Sex and ancient Indian women: Excerpts from Wendy Doniger's book', July 19 2015, *hindustantimes*. Retrieved from 2015https://www.hindustantimes.com/books/sex-and-ancient-indian-women-excerpts-from-wendy-doniger-s-book/story-mc841biatvNQ23mwcWOs2M.html

opinion. She doesn't care about the prevailing social norms or Maya.[52] (hence semi-nude and dark skin) her hair is never tied because you can never tame the Kali Goddess. She also has an outstretched tongue, Devdutt Pattanaik who writes on the relevance of mythology in modern times believes that perhaps Kali is trying to mock her devotees and sees right through their social facade and knows the dark desires that they are trying hard to suppress. She provokes them to look into their unconscious mind and face these memories.[53] A brief study of Kalika Puran tells us about how the ancient Indian society perceived women and she could be in her ultimate free form.

But this is not the same with Christianity who believed mother Mary to be Virgin and who was covered from top to bottom in clothes. It is therefore when British colonials came to India the Victorian values stigmatized Indian sexual liberalism because it was not according to the standards of 'Victorian morality'. They believed Indians and their values were too beastly and it was their (white man's burden) to make Indian society more civil & morally correct. The pluralism of Hinduism and its liberal attitudes were condemned as "barbaric" and proof of the inferiority of the East. The Indian Values of sexuality were despised and discussion about sex was seen as taboo.

Several movements were set up by prominent citizens, such as the Brahmo Samaj in Bengal and the Prarthana Samaj in Bombay Presidency, to work for the "reform" of Indian private

---

[52] https://faculty.chass.ncsu.edu/mgfosque/ENG219/Kali.html

[53] Devdutt Pattanaik, 'Kali and her tongue', *THE TIMES OF INDIA,* December 12, 2011. Retrieved from https://timesofindia.indiatimes. com/Kali-and-her-tongue/articleshow/10816142.cms

and public life[54]. Paradoxically, while this new consciousness led to the promotion of education for women and (eventually) a raise in the age of consent and reluctant acceptance of remarriage for widows, it also produced a puritanical attitude to sex even within marriage and the home.

European travellers to India in the 19th century were appalled by what they considered pornographic representations of sexual contact and intercourse on Hindu temples such as those of Khajuraho. Khajuraho was an ancient city in the Madhya Pradesh region of northern India. The majority of temples at Khajuraho were constructed between 950 and 1050 CE, The Kandariya Mahadeo temple is perhaps the most eye-catching building at Khajuraho and it is certainly the largest here there are richly developed erotic sculptures which include scenes of bestiality[55] and various acrobatic positions at these sculptures at Khajuraho that are symbolic and represent auspicious and protectiveness as well as fertility and happiness.

---

[54] Chakraborty, Kaustav, and Rajarshi Guha Thakurata. "Indian concepts on sexuality." Indian journal of psychiatry vol. 55,Suppl 2 (2013): S250-5doi:10.4103/0019-5545.105546, January 2013. Retrieved from https://www.ncbi.nlm.nih.gov/pmc/articles/PMC3705691/

[55] Tom Bartel, 'The Erotic Sculptures at Khajuraho, India', *Travel Past 50*, April 11, 2019. Retrieved from https://travelpast50.com/erotic-sculptures-khajuraho-india/

The Mithuna Figures – Khajuraho

Eroticism in ancient India was a well-studied concept as shown by the Kamasutra, written by Mallanaga Vatsyayana sometime during the 2nd or 5th century. It was considered to be an integral part of adult education at the time. However, with the discovery of new sea rout to India, major changes appear to have occurred following the British entry and drafting of the Indian Penal Code(IPC) by Lord Macaulay Wherein Indian culture was admixed with the Victorian system of ethical and moral standards. Subsequent growth of the pornography industry, fuelled by the recent advances in information and technology, has also further shaped the sex culture in India.

The 21st-century pornography industry is involved in the production and distribution of sexually explicit materials including literature, photos, audio, animation, movies, toys, and video games.

India witnessed the Commercialized Pornographic content in 1974, before this year Adult content like Adult Magazines and Erotica novels were available in every state but in regional languages and if anyone wanted to buy Premium Adult Magazines in English they had to order it from the United States after 1974 back issues of Playboy, Penthouse and Hustler had lost pride of place to indigenous products like Hot Wave, Confidential Adviser, Garam Kahaniyan (hot stories) and the seemingly innocuous For All and Film Mirror. Even today in 2020 Porn content in the localized language is openly sold at various railway stations and bus stands across India.

India saw the boon of Pictorial Prostitution only after 1995 when VSNL (Videsh Sanchar Nigam Limited) had formally launched the Internet for the Indian public.[56] Ever since then, Online porn has gone through a dramatic change. At that time to get an internet speed of 9.6 kbps, VSNL's rate was Rs. 5,000 and for 128 kbps was a whopping 30,000 lakhs.

In 2004, the government formulated its broadband policy, which defined broadband as "an always-on Internet connection with a download speed of 256 kbit/s (kilobits per second) or above." In 2010, the government auctioned 3G spectrum followed by the auction of the 4G spectrum that accelerated the pace of the wireless broadband market.

Today there is an ever-rising porn consumption in India due to cheaper data availability. At an average of 9.8GB per month, India has the world's highest data usage per phone. This number is expected to almost double to 18 GB by 2024, according to Swedish telecom equipment maker Ericsson.

According to a new report by adult website Pornhub, 89 percent Indians watched porn via mobile devices in 2019 – that is three percent more than the figure in 2017. The amount of users who consumed porn during the COVID19 lockdown in India is staggering.

---

[56] Leslie D'Monte, 'Evolving Internet in India', *livemint,* 18 Aug 2017. Retrieved from https://www.livemint.com/Opinion/gzWbpGZVD83 W3iq3uOLD7O/Evolving-Internet-in-India.html

There was a registered 20 percent jump in consuming porn content even before the official Lockdown in light of Covid 19 kicked in late March 2020. The fastest-growing Smartphone market showed a 95 % spike in traffic to adult sites during the first three week lockdown period[57], that too when the Indian administration has banned more than 3,500 porn websites in the country. Humanity has come far from clay figures to sculptures in temples to online Porn which is just a click-of-a-button away. The reality is, we are the first generation in the history of the world to be dealing with this on such a huge scale but the real question that we need to ask is where do we draw the line between Erotica and pervasive sex. Erotica has been used by people since ancient times. Then how do we determine whether it is moral or immoral? Especially when the notion of 'Morality' is highly dependent from person to person.

---

[57] 'Porn sites witnessed 95% spike in traffic in India during COVID-19 lockdown', *DNA*, May 6. 2020. Retrieved from https://www.dnaindia.com/india/report-porn-sites-witnessed-95-spike-in-traffic-in-india-during-covid-19-lockdown-2823803

Sexuality: Moral and Immoral

All human acts are subject to moral evaluation. Each knowingly chosen act is either good or evil, moral or immoral. There are also morally-neutral acts these include watching evening news, eating an apple instead of an orange etc. one cannot possibly classify these acts as moral or immoral. There are also moral obligatory acts which cast an obligation on an individual. For example, the duty to provide support, guidance and shelter to one's children.

Conversely, morals are the prevailing standards of behaviour that enable people to live cooperatively in groups. Moral refers to what societies sanction as right and acceptable.

Most people tend to act morally and follow societal guidelines. Morality often requires that people sacrifice their own short-term interests for the benefit of society. People or entities that are indifferent to right and wrong are considered amoral, while those who do evil acts are considered immoral.

While some moral principles seem to transcend time and culture, such as fairness, generally speaking, morality is not fixed. Morality describes the particular values of a specific group at a specific point in time. Historically, morality has been closely connected to religious traditions, but today its significance is equally important to the liberal world. For example, businesses and government agencies have codes of ethics that employees are expected to follow.

Some philosophers make a distinction between morals and ethics. But many people use the terms morals and ethics interchangeably when talking about personal beliefs, actions, or principles. So, morals are the principles that guide individual conduct within society. And, while morals may change over time, they remain the standards of behaviour that we use to judge right and wrong.

Morals and law at times go hand in hand, for instance, it's common to say, "My morals prevent me from cheating." It's also common to use ethics in this sentence instead. These morals are also incorporated in Contract law wherein once a contract of sale of goods is enforced the individuals involved are expected to not cheat or commit fraud if they do, then it will invite the legal penalty and in some cases even forfeiture of the contract. Hence here we see law and morals go hand in hand. However, there are instances where law and morals do not go hand in hand. In India living with your romantic partner without being married is immoral according to society. But the supreme court has given decision otherwise that, "to marry or not to marry or to have a heterosexual relationship is entirely personal." In Lata Singh v. State of UP [AIR 2006 SC 2522],[58] it was observed that a live-in relationship between two consenting adults of heterosexual

---

[58] M Katju, Supreme Court of India, 'Lata Singh vs State Of U.P. & Another', *Indiakanoon.org* Retrieved from https://indiankanoon.org/doc/1364215/

sex does not amount to any offence even though it may be perceived as immoral.

Indian ancient history gives many instances which the modern 21st-century Indian society will label immoral, evil or even forbidden for instance Erotica in India, which basically means the science of human creation. This science is mainly concerned with the fulfilment of the desires of the flesh.

Ancient Rigveda mentioned the Hymn to Creation the poet describes the time before creation. He then imagines that the primordial substance arose through the power of Tapas. The first product of the mind was the Kama, sexual desire, love, the bond between the non-existent and the existent. Eventually, this desire leads to the procreation and birth of beings, the Sages considered this as the primal source of all existence.

There are many instances which give us a glimpse about the sexuality of ancient Indian society. Ancient Hindu scriptures see sexuality from a broader perspective hence there are four goals of human life namely dharma (ethics), artha (wealth), kama (pleasure), and moksha (liberation).[59] As one goes through these Hindu scriptures one can easily find that different sexual activities can be classified as dharma sex, artha sex, kama sex, and moksha sex.

In dharma sex, the aim is to only procreate, hence in this type we don't see any attachment. The man will approach the woman with the sole intention of conceiving a child in her womb and this he can do only when the woman invites him since she understands her body better and knows when the period of ovulation will begin. Accordingly, when she approaches a

---

[59] Devdutt Pattanaik, 'Four Types of Sex', *Devdutt.com* 03rd April, 2014. Retrieved from https://devdutt.com/articles/four-types-of-sex/

suitable man he is bound to do his duty to copulate with her or he will be cursed. Rishis and their wives follow dharma sex. Kashyapa rishi is approached by Diti for copulation during his evening prayers. But he warns her by saying the child born out of this union will be Asuras, therefore, Hiranayaksha and Hiranakashipu are born. Kashyapa cannot refuse for sex as his wife has approached him during her ovulation period making sex a dharma or obligation.

In kama sex, the purpose is pleasure and nothing else. Kama is the god of desire who faces no defeat from anyone except Shiva that is why ironically Shiva is the fountain-head of Kama sutra. Kama sex will involve reaching the pinnacle of arousal and orgasm. Homosexuality falls into this category as sex can never lead to procreation. Kama is a powerful force that can distract the ambitious from his/her goal. Hence we can see that Vishnu takes the form of Mohini who is supposed to be a beautiful woman and lures and tricks the Asuras with pleasure and intimacy so that they are kept away from Amrit which would give them immortality.

Artha sees sex as a transaction, an exchange of services for goods. This type of sex is seen among courtesans and ganikas who provide sex as a service to men. Moksha sex on the other hand seeks to escape the cycle of birth and death. This idea is prevalent in Tantrik who do not associate with pleasure or procreation or service. Here sex is all about gaining powers which can control nature.[60]

Yam or Yamarāja is a Hindu God of death, the south direction, and the underworld, belonging to an early stratum of Rigvedic Hindu deities. He had a sister Yami. Rigveda gives an instance where Yami asks Yamraja to engage in sex with

---

[60] Ibid

him so that he can give her a child.[61] But her brother disagrees and upon refusal from Yamraj Yami insists that as a brother he should do his duty to give her a son.[62]

Vedas and Puranas were written by the Aryans who came to India in 2000 BC. Relationships prevalent during these times would have been labelled as beastly or incestuous by today's societal standard but these were pretty normal at the time. Aryans allowed their women to copulate between any of the class of devas for the sake of good breeding, so that the child born out of such relationship would have good genes.[63] In contrast to this Harivansh text which mentions about Brahmadev in the 3rd part of the book. Brahmadev the creator of the universe had a son Daksh, this son had a daughter who was given to Brahmadev and from this relationship they had a son who came to be known as Narada.[64]

The Mahabharata's 45th & 46th chapter of Adiparva mentions the conversation between Arjun & Urvashi.[65] Urvashi asks Arjun who is the archer and protagonist in Mahabharata war fought between brothers to satisfy her desire for pleasure, he denies as he is the son of Indradev and Urvashi was one of the Apsaras (Heavenly nymphs[66]) in Indradev's kingdom this makes Urvashi Arjun's Mother but she was adamant with

---

[61] Kalyanaraman Srinivasa, 'SEXUAL IMMORALITY OF ARYANS', *SPEAKINGTREE.IN*, February 20, 2014. Retrieved from https://www.speakingtree.in/blog/sexual-immorality-of-aryans

[62] pg.29 भारतीय विवाह संस्थेचा इतिहास, इतीहाचार्य वी. का. राजवाडे, प्रस्तावना - श्रीपाद अमृत डांगे

[63] Ibid

[64] pg. 32 Ibid

[65] pg 33 Ibid

[66] 'Apsaras, Apsarā, Apsara, Ap-sara: 15 definitions' *WISDOM LIBRARY*. Retrieved from https://www.wisdomlib.org/definition/apsaras

her demand she reckoned that in Indradev's kingdom there is sexual liberation and the Gods do not hesitate to satisfy her and that Arjun shouldn't too, but Arjun was reluctant to this offer and dismissed it. Because of this Urvashi got furious and cast a curse upon Arjun that if he does not satisfy her, the curse will make him a eunuch.

We can also see instances in ancient Hindu scriptures where the concept of monogamy was non-existent. This is exemplified from the fact that Krishna, an incarnation of Lord Vishnu had 16,108 wives. Similarly, another Draupadi was married to 5 characters namely Pandavas in Mahabharata.

There are also instances of bestiality in ancient society. Incest was not considered immoral in the Persian empire too. The Parthians and Persians married their own mothers. In ancient Persia, religion sanctified the union of a son with his mother. Incest in Ancient Egypt royal families was common and it was done to continue the purity of the race. Hinduism gives a broad meaning to sexuality and it seeks to strike a balance in life. Procreation and reproduction is seen as a continuation of the world. On the negative side, it admits the problem of egoism, selfishness, attachments, delusion, ignorance, bondage, etc., which may arise from unregulated sexual conduct.[67]

You might have heard about voyeurism, Gang-bang and swap culture in porn industries but this is not new to India. In 16th and 17th century Pune (Maharashtra) there was a type of sex game prevalent among the Peshwas who were one of the aristocrats of Maharashtra. The game was called as "Ghatakanchuki". In this game, a group of selected men would take brassieres worn by women and put it in a pot and

---

[67] 'Sexuality and Spirituality in Hinduism', *hinduwebsite.com* Retrived from https://www.hinduwebsite.com/editorial/sex-and-gurus.asp

randomly pick a brassiere from the pot. They would then have sex with whoever the brassiere belonged to. Historically this system was not only prevalent in Maharashtra but also in the Indian State of Karnataka.[68]

Sexual freedom was also recognized in ancient Greek city-states. Take the example of Zeus the Greek god, who wasted no time in establishing his dominance on Men as well as a women. He was a rather promiscuous god who raped multiple times. The Greek men were all bisexual, the private lives of men in the classical Athens the city of intellectuals was sexually liberating in the sense that men had relationships with adolescent boys too. Sex could be bought cheaply as the city was home to countless brothels[69]. but with the advance of science and culture, these practices were discontinued. Science has shown that child born from incest can have deformities and genetic defects; a classic example of this is King Tutankhamun from Egypt who was deformed as he was born out of incestuous marriage.

These days there are a lot of incestuous porn categories on the web you name it, they got it. "You can ask any young female porn performer what bookings she has this month, and she'll tell you she's playing 17 step-daughters,"[70] says Whitney Wright, who's filmed three performances for Pure Taboo, Since she came into the industry in 2016, the majority of her roles have involved some sort of family element. "Everybody has

---

[68] pg.36 भारतीय विवाह संस्थेचा इतिहास, इतीहाचार्य वी. का. राजवाडे, प्रस्तावना - श्रीपाद अमृत डांगे

[69] James Robson, 'The truth about sex in ancient Greece', *THE CONVERSATION*, April 1, 2015. Retrieved from https://theconversation.com/the-truth-about-sex-in-ancient-greece-39025

[70] Luke O'Neil, 'Incest Is the Fastest Growing Trend in Porn. Wait, What?' *esquire*, Feb 28, 2018. Retrieved from https://www.esquire.com/lifestyle/sex/a18194469/incest-porn-trend/

become pretty used to it." When we conducted an independent online survey about what type of porn people have seen least once we got the following data:

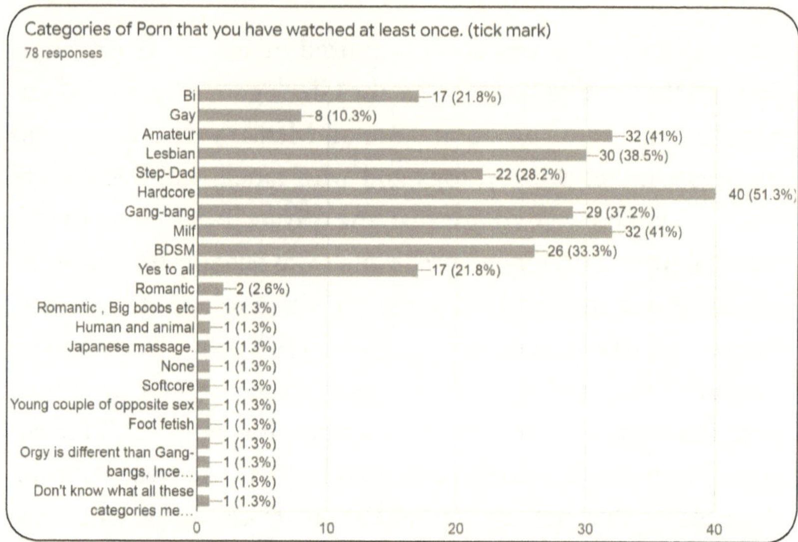

The more you look in Pornography that we have in the 21st century the deeper the rabbit hole goes. Could content of this kind really be reflecting our subconscious desires? If we think back to college psychology classes and consider Sigmund Freud's Oedipus complex theories, you could argue that watching incest porn is simply an act of wish fulfilment. Still, it feels like quite a stretch to assume that someone just typing in the most taboo sexual scenario they can think of into a porn search engine actually wants to have sex with a family member.[71] According to Freud, Oedipus complex is resolved as a child grows up, if a child fails to resolve he becomes fixated to his mother same is true for girl child who would be fixated

---

[71] Gareth May, 'Why Is Incest Porn So Popular?' *VICE*, February 25, 2015. Retrieved from https://www.vice.com/en_us/article/8gdz8k/why-is-incest-porn-so-popular-332

with her father if she fails to resolve. Could it be possible that these porn industries are actually profiting out of these psychological stages by introducing porn genres which depict mothers copulating with sons and daughters copulating with fathers?

A feminist pornographer Jacky St. James has embraced the controversial genre, calling it one of her favourites to direct. She says "These genres cannot be explored safely in real life"[72]. But mating with someone who shares a genetic profile too similar to yours (like a sibling or parent) leads to producing offspring with serious genetic abnormalities, which does nothing to help the survival instincts we're biologically wired with. One study found that people exposed to significant amounts of porn thought things like sex with animals and violent sex were twice as common as what those not exposed to porn believed. And when people believe a behaviour is normal, they're more likely to try it. One porn performer while interviewed by The Daily Beast said, "Some of my fans weren't nice anymore, they were creepy," she told The Daily Beast. "One fan told me that he and his wife conditioned their son his whole life until he was old enough to join them in bed. That really got to me. I almost felt like I was helping this kid get sexually abused."[73]

That said, scientists have also argued that we subconsciously use biological cues to estimate the relatedness of those around us, and if the relatedness is assumed to be too high, the very thought of any sexual relations with the person triggers innate incest avoidance mechanisms, a.k.a. disgust.

---

[72] Aurora Snow, 'Fauxcest': The Disturbing Rise of Incest-Themed Porn', *DAILY BEAST*, May. 05, 2017. Retrieved from https://www.thedailybeast.com/fauxcest-the-disturbing-rise-of-incest-themed-porn

[73] Ibid.

Speaking broadly pornography as well as prostitution work the same way--by selling a sexual pleasure. Is selling sex moral or immoral is a long debate going on since ages. prostitution is one of the oldest professions in the world, Sex workers who earn their living through this trade defend their identity while others like Catholic Sisters argue that there can be no dignity for sex sold for money. Meanwhile, Organizations like Human Rights Watch, the Global Alliance Against Traffic in Women, Global Commission on HIV and the Law, UNAIDS, and the World Health Organization had called for the decriminalisation of consensual sex work.[74] Some believe that what they do with their body is for them to decide as the idea of personal autonomy or sovereignty is a part of what it means to be a human, others like Doherty and sisters at the U.N. advocate that "prostitution is…perpetrated by patriarchy, misogyny, male privilege, sexism and gender-based violence." In my opinion, prostitution is based on two aspects that are consensual sex and contractual obligation. If both of these terms are met the state cannot impose its will to declare it immoral. Non-consensual sex and/or non-fulfilment of a contractual obligation which can involve trafficking, coercion and rape should call for a criminal penalty.

---

[74] Chris Herlinger, 'The worldwide debate about sex work: Morality meets reality', *globalsistersreport.org* Jul 27, 2017. Retrieved from https://www.globalsistersreport.org/news/trafficking/worldwide-debate-about-sex-work-morality-meets-reality-48216

Symbolism in Sexuality

Sexual attitudes and behaviours in ancient societies are indicated by art, literature and inscriptions, and to a lesser extent by archaeological remains such as erotic artefacts and architecture (as seen in Khajuraho Temple). We try to explore our sexuality through erotic content, novels, romantic partner or porn although we still don't know a lot about sexual fantasies there are hundreds of genres in porn and adult content. Although most of these genres might seem modern, most of them were in fact fantasies of the humans we walked the earth in ancient times.

What turns you on in porn depends on what you have experienced in the past. Many people who had repressed masturbation and continued attaching feelings of shame to it previously may find masturbation shaming a turn on. but as PhD sexologist Dr. Jessica O'Reilly in an interview with Vice Media points out, "not all your porn preferences stem from something in your past." "Something that's exciting for many people is simply the idea of getting something you're not supposed to have, or something that is not available for you".[75]

According to Ashley Cowie a Writer and Filmmaker, "Early cultures associated having sex with supernatural forces and religious architecture and arts which are intertwined with such depictions. Sexual imagery is found on statues, pottery, paintings, sculpture, dramatic arts, religious buildings, monuments and music. Thousands of years before the written word ancient societies extended their sexuality and sexual practices into the surrounding landscapes. At important dates in agricultural and ritual calendars, people got hyper-sexualised and spiritualised at natural places perceived as being abundant with the magic energy of fertilisation."[76]

Cowrie shells a type of seashells symbolize vagina because it is roughly shaped in the form of a vagina. Cowrie shells are often worn as charms against sterility. To solemnize a relationship between a man and a woman there are marriage ceremonies there are many symbols which are fertility charms hence cowrie shell which is a charm against sterility is quite naturally an important part of marriage.[77]

In some Indian societies there exists a custom of "Dej" in which gifts and goods are exchanged between the families of

---

[75] Sierra Bein, 'What Your Favorite Porn Genre Says About You Three sexologists offer competing theories on why you keep searching for crossdressing, MILFs, or cartoons.', *VICE*, May 26, 2017. Retrieved from https://www.vice.com/en_us/article/zmbdq5/what-your-favourite-porn-genre-says-about-you

[76] Ashley Cowie, 'SEX SYMBOLS OF THE ANCIENT WORLD', *ashleycowie.com*, March 16, 2017. Retrieved from https://ashleycowie.com/blog/sex-symbols-of-the-ancient-world#:~:text=Mountains%2C%20hills%2C%20rivers%2C%20waterfalls,importantly%20to%20assure%20the%20daily

[77] Pg.68 लज्जागौरी, रा. ची. ढेरे.

husband and bride in these customs the exchange of cowrie shells is important for instance in Andhra Pradesh, there is a community in Erkal where cowrie shells are given to the father in law to observe the custom of Dej. In Rajasthan during marriage ceremonies the bride wears traditional attire on the day of the wedding, during the marriage ceremony in the mandap some customary material is hung and cowrie is also an important part of it. Similarly, cowrie has customary importance in the Indian states of Maharashtra and Orissa too.[78]

In India, even mere mention of menstruation has become a taboo in the past and even to this date the cultural and social influences appear to be a hurdle for the advancement of knowledge on the subject. Culturally in many parts of India, menstruation is still considered to be dirty and impure but this was not the case in ancient India. With the advent of western education, especially when the British colonizers came to Indian subcontinent Hindus were made to feel that this whole ceremony is horrendous – how can you announce that your daughter has now started menstruating, what an embarrassment, how orthodox, what a shameful ritual, how backward – these were the things we were told. In Bengal, it is believed that at the first burst of rain mother earth prepared herself for being fertilized by menstruating. During that time there is an entire cessation from all ploughing, sowing and other farm work. The menstruation of the Earth Goddess is thus observed by the Bengali as a Sabbath.

In tantric rituals, there is a type of worship known as Yoni Puja (worship of the female Vagina). Here the association of

---

[78] pg.69 Ibid.

menstruation with sacredness is reinforced, wherein ritual worship is carried out not only of a woman but also of her Yoni or Vagina, which is perceived to be a symbol of the Cosmic Yoni from which the entire universe has emerged. According to Tantric philosophy menstrual blood is, in fact, considered pure and sacred, and plays a very important role in these Tantric rituals.

In Yoni Tantra, the Yoni puja mandates that the puja must be carried only in a yoni which has begun menstruating. It says: "The yoni which has bled is suitable for worship. Do not worship a yoni which has never bled. Worshipping a yoni which has never bled causes loss of siddhi on every occasion."[79]

In Travancore, there is an important ceremony known as 'Trippukharattu' or purification ceremony, in connection with the menstruation of the goddess, which is believed to take place about eight or ten times a year, in which a cloth wrapped around the mental image of the goddess is found to be discoloured with red spots and is subsequently in demand as a holy relic.

In my primary school, I was often intrigued by how human babies were born. How do women get pregnant? Who puts the baby inside her, how does it get inside her and how is the baby born? My childhood friend Ramesh (name changed) had answers, he was the smart kid in the school and teachers loved Ramesh for he was their pet student as he always got good grades and did his homework daily. Most importantly Ramesh had answers to my question. He told me when a man and woman are married God comes down from heaven to the

---

[79] Nithin Sridhar, 'Some sects of Hinduism encourage sex during your periods' *ThePrint*, 3 February, 2019. Retrieved from https://theprint.in/pageturner/excerpt/some-sects-of-hinduism-encourage-sex-during-your-periods/186312/

house of this young couple and puts his hand on the womb of the lady, her stomach bloats and voila! she's pregnant. I do not remember if I believed in God or not at such a young age but for a student who despised the primary school, I always prayed to God to give me more holidays. Anyway, I was not satisfied with the answer. I came home and asked my mom the same question. She told me I was too young to understand this concept and as I become older she'll explain the whole process to me.

It was only much later in my high school that I came to know how babies are born and I came to know this not from Ramesh or mom but from another group of friends(who introduced me to porn). Meanwhile, my interest in history also taught me that ancient Indian societies were not so embarrassed to discuss sex for instance look at how we worship Shiva the Indian God. The first evidence of Shiva comes from the pre-Vedic era, from a seal from the Indus Valley civilisation. It shows a naked man with an erect penis, sitting in the yogic "throne" position or Bhadrasana, wearing horned headgear, surrounded by animals.[80] Most scholars opine that it is an early form of Shiva, which captures his three attributes that is Shiva as Pashupati, lord of animals; as Yogeshwara, lord of yoga; and as Lingeshwara, lord of the phallus.

Shiva is known as Rudra in early Vedic scriptures which are conservatively dated 1500 BCE,. Rudra, the god of the roaring storm, is usually portrayed in accordance with the element he represents as a fierce and one who brings destruction. He is a

---

[80] 'Why is Shiva represented by a sexual symbol, asks a new book', *scroll. in.* Retrieved from https://scroll.in/article/833935/why-is-shiva-represented-by-a-sexual-symbol-asks-a-new-book

God who is feared hence It is no surprise that he is seen as a god who howls and shoots arrows that spread disease.[81]

Shiva's phallic representation in the form of shiv ling has made Hindus embarrassed, many still don't believe that it symbolises the phallus.

Phallic worship is common in many mythologies. And it is typically associated with fertility (more children, more crops, more fruits, more cows, more horses, and more sheep). It is also used to ward away troublesome spirits, frighten them. Hinduism considers the lingam and yoni together to symbolize the union of the male and female principles and the totality of all existence.[82] Shiva is also said to be the source of the Kama-sutra and in the Kumara-sambhava, Kalidasa's Sanskrit poem on the birth of Shiva's son is rather erotic.[83]

In ancient Egypt, Min was considered to be a god of fertility and harvest, the embodiment of the masculine principle depicted with an erect phallus. For centuries, Bhutan has celebrated the phallus. They are painted on homes, or carved in wood, installed above doorways and under eaves to ward off evil.[84] Today, if you travel to Bhutan, you will find penis

---

[81] Ibid

[82] Matt Stefon, 'Lingam Hindu symbol', *Britannica.* Retrieved from https://www.britannica.com/topic/lingam

[83] Devdutt Pattanaik, 'Do Hindus worship the phallus? Keep calm (about Hinduism) and ask Devdutt.' *dailyO,* 15-08-2016. Retrieved from https://www.dailyo.in/lifestyle/devdutt-pattanaik-phallus-shiva-hinduism-mythology-gods-fertility/story/1/12380.html

[84] Steven Lee Myers, 'Phallus Art Brings Luck in Bhutan—and Tourists, Too', *The New York Times,* August 24, 2017. Retrieved from https://www.nytimes.com/2017/08/24/world/asia/bhutan-phallus-commercialization-tourism.html#:~:text=LOBESA%2C%20Bhutan%20E2%80%94%20For%20centuries%2C,as%20a%20kind%20of%20scarecrow.

statues being sold as good-luck charms and bad-luck-warders on the street.

If we learn sex in its true sense and how the ancient Indians interpreted it and how modern society interprets it now we arrive at a completely different Conclusion.

How Porn Has Wired Our Brain

The internet is a double-edged sword on one hand with the aid of Globalization it has revolutionized trade and communication. With the faster speed of the internet, Doctors can perform surgeries from any end of the world. Take a moment to think how well we are connected to our friends and family owing to Snapchat, WhatsApp, Instagram and Facebook every day we are constantly in contact with one another through one or more of the Social Media platforms. On the other hand, many have become emotionally dependent on the internet to fulfil their deepest desires.

A hundred years ago we were told masturbation would make you go blind but it's safe to say that our society has progressed in the field of science and this statement holds no ground. Research has shown that masturbation can help you relieve stress and also improve self-esteem.[85] Some researchers also believe that the endorphins released during masturbation

---

[85] 'Is Masturbation Healthy?' *Planned Parenthood. Retrieved from* https://www.plannedparenthood.org/learn/sex-pleasure-and-sexual-dysfunction/masturbation/masturbation-healthy#:~:text=Masturbation%20can%20actually%20be%20good,and%20make%20you%20feel%20good.

can help reduce painful menstrual cramps.[86] When I was in my High School there was a popular rumour around when the boys hit puberty at 13 that if they masturbated frequently we would not get acne. Elders or seniors wouldn't talk about sex and our only way of understanding our body because of the changes it was going through was…you guessed it right porn.

In India, over the last five years, we have had overwhelming content on Indian online streaming platforms. Anveshi Jain who appeared in Gandii Baat, a web series on Ekta Kapoor's streaming platform ALTBalaji while speaking to Vice Media said "I know why I have such a huge following," she tells VICE India in an interview. "It's because of my physical traits because I am heavily bosomed. It took me a long time to get used to this idea but I am not going to lie to myself anymore."

Another online streaming platform which allows customers to watch a wide variety of Web Series, Ullu, was launched around the same time as Jain. Since most Indians are confined to their house during lockdown indulging in hobbies, joining online courses and binge-watching shows and movies that they had planned, the internet saw a spike in traffic not only on Netflix and Amazon Prime but also some digital platforms that stream adult content like "Ullu". The most popular series on this platform are Charamsukh, Panchali and Kavita Bhabhi.[87]

---

86 Clár McWeeney, 'Masturbating during your period', *helloclue.com,* January 30, 2018. Retrieved from https://helloclue.com/articles/sex/masturbating-during-your-period

87 'Indian Adult Content App Launches New Plans, Minimise Subscription Rates as India Watches More Explicit Shows Amid Lockdown', March 26, 2020. Retrieved from https://www.india.com/entertainment/indian-adult-content-app-launches-new-plans-minimise-subscription-rates-as-india-watches-more-explicit-shows-amid-lockdown-3981702/

Originally the platform was launched only in Indian but because of lockdown, it has gained popularity worldwide.

This explicit content is getting popular because it is well received by the Indian audience and has led to other digital platforms like Zee5 and Voot to create their own erotica series and inspired the launch of several copycat apps like KooKu, PrimeFlix and Hotshots.

Director Sachin Mohite who directed *Gaandi Baat* while speaking to Vice Media said: "the series found an audience because it talks about all the things we find difficult to openly discuss". "We pass them off as 'gandi baat' (obscene talk)," he says. He recounts the story of a friend who was insecure about her body. "She feared her boyfriend would lose interest in sex because she was flat-chested but couldn't discuss it with anyone." Mohite used this as a subplot in one of the episodes of the series. "These are the kind of stories we tell without being preachy."[88]

Today the porn sector is worth billions of dollars. It's no surprise that in the lockdown period there has been a 95% increase in people consuming porn in India. Sigmund Freud the Father of psychology believed that people's naturally strong instincts toward sexuality were repressed by people to meet the constraints imposed on them by civilized life. These repressed sexual impulses are satisfied by the porn industries. porn has no limits what may be considered taboo or immoral is vividly fantasized, exaggerated, and fetishized in videos and is readily available at the click of the button.

---

[88] By Dipti Nagpaul, 'Why Are Local Indian Streaming Platforms So Full of Erotic Content? An Investigation', *VICE*, 01 July 2020. Retrieved from https://www.vice.com/en_in/article/ep4pep/indian-local-streaming-platforms-erotica-sex

In 2016 the analytics report of just one website, Pornhub, revealed that its videos were watched 92 billion times last year, by 64 million daily visitors.[89] If we try to calculate these videos it comes to 12.5 videos for every person on the planet, and if you tried to watch all of them, you'd be busy for 524,641 years continuously.

Just as the tobacco industry argued for decades that there was no proof of a connection between smoking and lung cancer, so, too, has the porn industry. but the real question to be asked is how does pornography affect our brain to make us an addict because historically we have seen every age had their own erotic and pornographic symbols, sculptures and paintings so were these people addicted why is the modern online porn a hot topic to talk about?

Pornography addiction is much more involved than just wanting to look at nude videos and pictures it has gone much beyond pleasure. It has a deep connection to our learning process and the chemicals in our brain. Your brain on porn is much more complicated than you think.

---

[89] Guy Kelly, 'The scary effects of pornography: how the 21st century's acute addiction is rewiring our brains', *The Telgraph*, 11 September 2017. Retrieved from https://www.telegraph.co.uk/men/thinking-man/scary-effects-pornography-21st-centurys-accute-addiction-rewiring/

Porn and Mental Health

Ever since the big bang and subsequent expansion of the universe, the earth saw life forms which multiplied and mutilated overtime. Whether it is algae, insect-eating plants, trees, rodents or the annoying mosquito which bites you at night or seaweed that stinks up our summer beaches all are by-products of evolutionary sex. These lineages go back nearly 2 billion years. But it took another 1.5 billion years for the sex to evolve as we know it today, I am talking about the type of sex humans have with penetrating the male organ into the female vagina i.e. internal fertilization. This sex is seen among reptiles, Fish, birds and mammals too.

Something about copulation must be so rewarding that all the organisms engage in it. Is it a continuation of their species? yes. Reproduction makes sure that the animal breed does not get extinct but more and more research is coming out which says even animals engage in sex without reproduction. To say all living beings have sex for the continuation of their species would be incorrect because we'd be completely ignoring the pleasurable part of it. Animals also enjoy pleasure for instance psychologists Jeffrey Burgdorf and Jaak Panksepp discovered that laboratory rats enjoyed being tickled, emitting a sort of chirpy laugh outside the range of human hearing. But does that include Carnal pleasure too? Bonobos a type of monkeys showed that they had plenty of sex even though when the pregnancy was impossible, they engaged in carnal pleasure after giving birth to individuals. This means if animals have sex without the intention of procreation, they have a pleasure-driven motivation. A female lion will mate roughly 50times per day over a week and it just takes one sperm to fertilize the egg. This type of sex among animals is seen among other species of leopards and cougars too and not to forget same-sex sexual behaviour, which is definitional non-reproductive, occurs in every vertebrate and few non-vertebrate organisms like fruit flies of bed bugs. Oral sex also occurs in some species. Reproduction is so important in terms of the continuation of species that nature has made it very pleasurable for – humans as well as – animals and both seek this pleasure actively without feeling the necessity to reproduce every time.[90]

These days one can get sexual pleasure by looking at xxx-rated images and videos. Some people even argue that these images and videos help them to eradicate sexual stigma and reduce shame. Well, they are not wrong, porn can also be a good source of entertainment. Similarly, it can also help you to understand what turns you on. How can we forget that mainstream porn has given rise to queer diverse indie porn? As opposed to dirty magazines which were mostly for the heterosexuals, 21st-century porn offers tons of sex-positive, feminist, queer, indie, hairy, non-binary, body-positive,

---

[90] Jason G Goldman, 'Do animals have sex for pleasure? We thought we were the only species to enjoy intimate interactions, but as Jason G Goldman discovers, a few curious couplings in nature have changed our view.', *BBC*, 13th June 2014. Retrieved from https://www.bbc.com/future/article/20140613-do-animals-have-sex-for-fun

and ethical porn to choose from. This is a form of art and expression that people can easily access to satisfy their pleasure and have a great orgasm without the need to wear protection or feeling awkward. Porn is liberating one can watch it without any repercussions…or is it?

Whether it is incestuous porn, Amateur or softcore. Research shows that pornography hijacks the pleasure centre of your brain. It floods your neural-network with dopamine. Which is to say, the more you watch pornography the harder it is to find happiness outside of pornography. So do people who frequently view pornography are more prone to depression? Or do depressed people are more prone to view pornography? Dr. Kevin B Skinner answers this question in *Psychology Today* he conducted a survey of nearly 450 people in which 30 percent reported that they view pornography at least three to five times a week and over 25 percent indicate that they view pornography daily.

In our own Indian survey, we found out that 70% of individuals gave an affirmative answer when asked if their close friends consume porn.

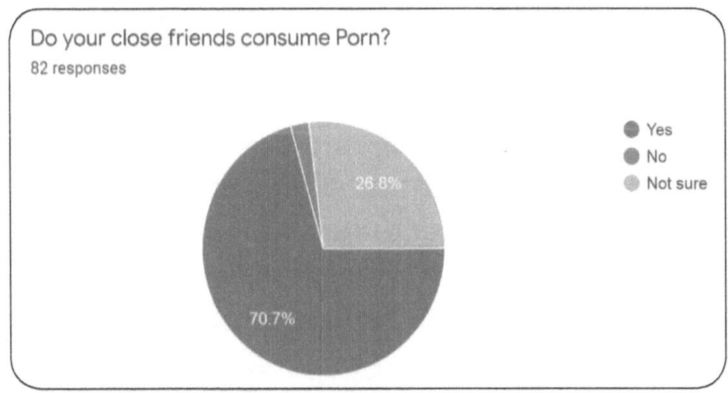

One of the people who took our Google online survey about how pornography affects the brain was asked if sex education is important she said "All I knew about sex when I was younger was from my colony friends who were older than me, and all that they've told me has turned out to be false"

"If I had a reliable source it would've been much better for me and probably wouldn't require porn. Thankfully I'm not half as addicted to porn as I have a healthy sex life, and may watch it like once a month to learn new moves, but things aren't same for some of my friends who watch porn and masturbate every day."

The Coronavirus Pandemic forced various countries to declare a lockdown to contain the situation and stop the spread of the Virus. This Pandemic has forced people to face some ugly truths of life. As Covid 19 kept people at home, Indians increasingly went online in pursuit of gratification, "Work from home" has pushed office work inside home boundaries. Quint media report suggested that "Globally, half (51 percent) of employees admitted watching more adult content on the same devices they use for work-related purposes".[91] Overall Indians seem to be leading the world in porn consumption because reports show a 95 percent spike in traffic to adult sites during the lockdown period. The hike in consumption of adult content can be seen not only in India but also in European countries, the United States and South Korea. During this period Pornhub went one step further and took to Twitter to announce that in a bid to help "flatten the curve", they will extend their Free Premium content worldwide until April 23 2020. The popular porn website said in its tweet, "Stay home and help flatten the curve! Since COVID-19 continues to

---

[91] IANS, 'People Admit To Watching Porn on Same Device Used For Work: Report', *the Quint,* 06 May 2020. Retrieved from https://www. thequint.com/tech-and-auto/tech-news/people-admit-watching-porn-on-same-device-used-for-work-from-home

impact us all, Pornhub has decided to extend Free Pornhub Premium worldwide until April 23rd. So enjoy, stay home, and stay safe Fire #StayHomehub." Corey Price, Pornhub's vice president, said in a statement, "With nearly one billion people in lockdown across the world because of the coronavirus pandemic, it's important that we lend a hand and provide them with an enjoyable way to pass the time. We hope by expanding our offer of free Pornhub Premium worldwide, people have an extra incentive to stay home and flatten the curve."[92]

Oftentimes consumers encounter porn accidentally or a friend introduces it to them, consumers have also reported that they liked cyberporn more than they had expected. A research conducted in The Journal for Sexual Medicine categorised heterogeneous populations who consumed porn into recreational, highly distressed non-compulsive, and compulsive use. In this, Recreational which constituted 75% of the total users reported higher sexual satisfaction and lower sexual compulsivity, avoidance, and dysfunction, whereas users with a compulsive profile presented lower sexual satisfaction and dysfunction and higher sexual compulsivity and avoidance.[93] The problem is not in watching porn itself but what effects it

---

[92] 'Pornhub is Giving out 'Free Premium' to Encourage People to Stay at Home amid Corona Lockdown', *NEWS 18*, March 25 2020. Retrieved from https://www.news18.com/news/buzz/pornhub-is-giving-out-free-premium-to-encourage-people-to-stay-at-home-amid-corona-lockdown-2550601.html

[93] Vaillancourt-Morel, Marie-Pier & Blais-Lecours, Sarah & Labadie, Chloé & Bergeron, Sophie & Sabourin, Stéphane & Godbout, Natacha. (2016). Profiles of Cyberpornography Use and Sexual Well-Being in Adults. The Journal of Sexual Medicine. 14. 10.1016/j.jsxm.2016.10.016. Retrieved from https://www.researchgate.net/publication/311782345_Profiles_of_Cyberpornography_Use_and_Sexual_Well-Being_in_Adults

has on the body. When a user seeks ever more intense levels of stimulation, more edgy stuff, and is getting bored with the usual fare, the use might be problematic. Also If you have a willing partner who wants to have sex but you prefer porn over sex this might be problematic.

Porn consumers will tell you they watch it to spice up their relationship. Yes, watching porn can allow couples to explore sexual activities that they may be curious about. Then there are Porn industries which will tell you Pornography is the new hot entertainment out there and there is absolutely no harm in viewing it, they will further go on to tell you that for every two thousand videos you watch they will do charity to save whales in the ocean. Ironically, these are the same websites which will feature categories like "teen crying," "gagging," "forced sex," while others have genre like "toothless granny porn", "garden gnomes" in which the pointed hat is used as a buttplug(yikes). Consumers are also more prone to addictions when they do certain things secretly. They have nobody to whom they will hold accountability and nobody knows about their compulsive habit. Consumers addicted to porn don't feel the need to have a social life or a real physical and emotional relationship with anyone.

In research published by *Psychology Today*, it was found that: Individuals who view pornography daily scored in the severe depression range (over 21) while those who viewed porn three to five times a week averaged a little above 15; still not great but not severe depression.[94]

---

[94] Kevin B Skinner Ph.D, 'Can Pornography Trigger Depression?', *Psychology Today*, November 03, 2011. Retrieved from https://www.psychologytoday.com/intl/blog/inside-porn-addiction/201111/can-pornography-trigger-depression

Porn and Depression are vicious cycles. People who watch porn can get depression and people who are depressed may start watching it as a way to escape their problems.[95] Pornography can create, agitate, and trap you in depression and anxiety.[96] As studies have shown porn burns out dopamine receptors, leaving you feeling more helpless. And porn can trap you in depression by draining you of life, instead of fulfilling the promise of giving you life.

Delayed gratification is a crucial skill to learn if one is to maintain control and direction in their life. Delaying gratification isn't a new concept. Back in 300 B.C, Aristotle tried to study why so many people were unhappy in their lives he concluded that it was because they confused pleasure for true happiness.[97] Basically, the healthiest of individuals have mastered the art of discipline and delayed gratification. Aristotle said true happiness is developing habits and surrounding yourself with people who grow your soul, which will allow you to move towards your greatest potential. Repeatedly giving in to the urge to watch pornography leads to a lack of ability to delay gratification. Your brain becomes more and more focused on the things you find pleasurable and the discipline of delayed gratification falls to the wayside. There is a certain sense of superiority and confidence that comes with the realization that

---

[95] Ibid.

[96] By: Shane James O'Neill, 'MENTAL HEALTH, DEPRESSION, SUICIDE, AND PORNOGRAPHY', *PROVENMEN*, January 31, 2019. Retrieved from https://www.provenmen.org/mental-health-depression-suicide-pornography-2/

[97] Ilene Strauss Cohen Ph.D, 'The Benefits of Delaying Gratification Are you avoiding pain or living with purpose?' *Psychology Today*, December 26, 2017. Retrieved from https://www.psychologytoday.com/us/blog/your-emotional-meter/201712/the-benefits-delaying-gratification

you have more control over your primal desires, something that porn users lack.[98]

Video is powerful and Prolonged use of these porn videos produces habituation. We live in a world where we need to see something to believe it and in our fast-paced, information-driven world, video is the preferred means of communication and information dissemination. Sight, sound, and motion can be a powerfully positive combination. This is why companies in today's competitive environment spend billions of dollars on video advertisements, there are so many advertisements which we have seen in our childhood on TV and still, remember the music and scenes even after 10-15 years. It wouldn't be wrong to say that video has the power to influence and even replace behaviours in your mind without you being consciously aware of what you are seeing.

As you watch videos, your subconscious mind is rapidly dissecting, translating and making sense of what it is being fed. The research has found that the subconscious mind translates and subsequently changes our behaviour in one disturbing way:

Pornography teaches us promiscuity and sex with multiple partners, this downgrades our standards sexually. It encourages us to seek unhealthy relationships with people who are willing to have sex without any boundaries. In addition to that, In India, there is no education policy to provide formal sex education to adolescents hundreds of hours of porn create certain expectations of what sex looks like. The average

---

[98] This article was originally published in the Elephant Journal by J.K Emezi. It has been edited for content and clarity by fightthenewdrug. org '5 Ways Porn Can Harm Your Brain, Body, And Quality Of Life', *fightthenewdrug.org* March 24, 2020. Retrieved from https:// fightthenewdrug.org/5-ways-porn-changes-your-brain-and-body-for-the-worse/

16-year-old consuming pornography is literally getting his or her sex education from the videos he/she watches. And that's not good, especially because porn sells a warped fantasy and exaggerated reality of what real sex is like.

Since porn subdues the reward mechanism you will never come across someone dependent on porn who was great at goal setting. most people who abuse pornography usually also struggle in their finances, relationships, and careers it is no surprise that porn causes lethargy.

Over 500 million people scroll down their Instagram feed each day photoshopped bodies of Instagram models set unrealistic standards. The media often favours one "ideal" body type, based on strongly gendered ideas of masculine or feminine. Pornography, These bodies and body shapes do not look like most people. In fact, trying to reach that size or shape would be impossible or very unhealthy for many people! The actors in porn often go through a lot of surgeries to enhance their bodies using Botox and silicon. This is also a problem with porn, as porn stars also often have unrealistic bodies.

When we see the same types of images over and over, we may start to believe they're normal or real. This distorted perception of reality can lead to people feeling unhappy about their body or having low self-esteem. These standards set by porn about the size of penises, breasts, buttocks and so on might not be achievable for everyone, as a matter of fact, and it might also be unhealthy. When I talked to gay men and heterosexual women they said the size of the penis never really mattered as a person. People who have a big penis do not automatically become good in bed.

Confession of Ex-Porn Addicts

In 2015 when Ministry of Information and Broadcasting released a notification in India for service providers to ban pornography. As a rebellious teenager, it struck my freedom of speech and expression nerve. Being a law student my pro-constitution morality was immediately activated, I debated with my friends and professors,

"How can the government stop an individual from watching explicit material within the four walls of his house, isn't it an invasion of privacy and personal liberty?"

"This is nothing but a sheer violation of Article 19(1)(a) of the Indian constitution", I said to myself.

As I was reading about the topic since then, finding out the risk-to-benefit ratio of viewing pornography was topping the ranks of controversial topics. It is when I often pondered upon these questions, "Addictions about porn aside, in-general can porn consumption be healthy?" "Can people be smart enough to watch it in regulation?"

It is important to ask these questions because we need to look at the other side and without doing that we won't be able to understand pornography, sexuality and dopamine completely; besides any research is prone to cognitive biases and by cognitive bias I mean if I were to find out a definitive conclusion to, let's say "people prefer Marvel comics over DC comics" then if I am an Ironman fan I would subconsciously only look at those studies which support Marvel comics and prove that people do in fact prefer Marvel comics over DC comics since there are more number of the audience watching Marvel movies in theatres than DC. This would mean my research is biased because I failed to take into account if people watch DC comics, movies, and series on platforms like Television channels, Amazon Prime and Netflix. Scientific methodology through research should be aimed at avoiding these cognitive errors or preferring one comic over the other or confirmatory bias. To understand this we must realise that humans are prone to biases which leads to error. The more I am anticipating the outcome the more I am likely to make an error. To be honest I suck at weighing evidence but that is alright because psychology says we all do. In fact, confirmation bias which makes humans prone to outcome-driven research is well documented in cognitive literature in psychology.

Then we arrive at how we get rid of these cognitive biases so that our research is "pure and unbiased." The answer lies in scientific methods which are designed precisely to avoid these cognitive errors. In the words of Feynman, "Science is what we do to keep us from lying to ourselves". The scientific methodology aims to neutralise the effects of these biases and thereby reduce error. We can say that an argument for research is true when we have a compelling argument for accepting the authority of science, especially where there is a **consensus on the issue among the relevant experts in the mainstream scientific community.**

Now, back to the original question: "Addictions about porn aside, in-general can porn consumption be healthy?" "Can people be smart enough to watch it in regulation?"

Pornography in itself is not inherently harmful to men or women.[99] Some people can watch porn occasionally and not suffer significant side effects. However, what also must be stressed is that there is an increasing number of teens with plastic brains who prefer online eporn over sexuality.[100] If you visit YourBrainOnPorn.com and Reddit's No Fap online community you will see stories from thousands of young people struggling to overcome what they feel is an escalating compulsion. Excessive porn viewing often presents another unaddressed health problem like Anxiety and Depression or Bi-polar disorder. When people get lonely and/or are depressed they may find relief through masturbation in a way to calm themselves in these cases porn is the symptom and not the cause. When these mental health issues are not present pornography can be helpful. In fact, sometimes Counselors suggest porn to help people become comfortable with a fantasy they or their partner may have. And yet there also those researchers who say that basic psychological science suggests

---

[99] Candida Royalle, Pornography Can Be Good for Consumers', *The New York Times,* November 11, 2012. Retrieved From https://www.nytimes.com/roomfordebate/2012/11/11/does-pornography-deserve-its-bad-rap/pornography-can-be-good-for-consumers#:~:text=When%20none%20of%20these%20red,with%20what%20turns%20you%20on.

[100] Philip Zimbardo Ph.D, 'Is Porn Good for Us or Bad for Us? New research suggests watching porn may lead to some undesirable consequences.' Mar 01, 2016. Retrieved from https://www.psychologytoday.com/us/blog/hero/201603/is-porn-good-us-or-bad-us

frequent exposure to porn may indeed lead to normalization of harmful behaviours.

In another study by researchers at the University of Cambridge found that men who demonstrate compulsive sexual behaviour that is an excessive preoccupation with sexual fantasies, urges or behaviours that is difficult to control, causes you distress, or negatively affects your health, job, relationships or other parts of your life required more sexual images than their peers.[101] Let's look at some of the people who were once addicted to this imagery:

Terry Crews – Actor

Terry, a Hollywood actor who has worked in popular Netflix series like Brooklyn 99, was a porn addict since the age of 12. While giving an interview to a T.V channel Terry said growing up in childhood his dad was an alcoholic and mother a strict Christian who was addicted to religion and would put too many restrictions on Terry and his siblings.[102] His only get away from his problems – Porn. Terry would go over to his Uncle's basement to watch porn and escape reality. Terry says the fact that people don't know about your porn addiction makes it more insidious. He had this crippling addiction till he got married and it is when he realized that it had started affecting his marriage he knew this was going way out of his hand that is when he decided to quit

---

[101] Banca P, Morris LS, Mitchell S, Harrison NA, Potenza MN, Voon V. Novelty, conditioning and attentional bias to sexual rewards. J Psychiatr Res. 2016;72:91-101. doi:10.1016/j.jpsychires.2015.10.017. Retrieved from https://pubmed.ncbi.nlm.nih.gov/26606725/

[102] *tjsmith*. 'Terry Crews talks about his Porn Addiction' Youtube Retrieved from: https://youtu.be/xxmqmcdXV8I

porn by going to a rehab centre. Terry thinks pornography encourages us to view people as objects and nothing more than body parts out of which we extract pleasure rather than people to be loved.

Candace Bure – Actress

While speaking to The View Candance said Pornographic images are harder to get out of your system than drugs like Cocaine because cocaine can be flushed out of your system while porn stays in your mind. She says the first time when she was exposed to pornography she was 12 years old and she can still see it and it's something that she cannot forget, pornography is available easily to kids she says and that is such a perversion of what sex should be like.

Russel Brand – Comedian

According to him, Pornography reduces the spectacle of sex to an extracted physical act. Russel was obsessed with porn as a teenager but back then getting access to porn was a huge task as he had to hide magazines and other content related to porn to have access to it but now it is available so easily over a Wi-Fi he says. He says porn users will never feel after watching the porn that damn! What a productive time I have spent connecting to the world!

The feeling which one gets while watching porn is that I am doing something wrong which gets worse into a feeling of guilt and shame after you have ejaculated. Russel says porn was affecting his ability to relate to women and relating to him and his sexuality. He says the direction that we ought to go in is how can we understand our sexuality and how can we express it lovingly.

Jada Smith – Actress

Jada while speaking to Entertainment Tonight said she had an unhealthy relationship with porn.[103] When asked what made her watch porn she replies that it came from an emotional place she was feeling empty back then when she had started to watch it she was also single. Jada thinks Porn gives the user a false expectation that a woman is ever ready to engage in coitus this creates an unrealistic expectation in men and women. I absolutely love Jada smith because no topic is completely off the limits for discussion when it comes to Jada.

---

[103] 'Jada Pinkett Smith Opens Up About Past Porn Addiction', *Entertainment Tonight.* Youtube. Retrieved from https://youtu.be/ mKOzKHrA6b0

Porn Rehab Centres

Back in the 19th century if someone complained that he was addicted to smoking cigarettes, people would have not believed him, smoking was not considered a terrible vice and rehabilitation centres during this time were almost non-existent. Then the 20th century came in when we saw the rise of capitalists bourgeoising their Cigarette propaganda on the world. Doctors and pharmacists were hired and paid royalties to make smoking the new normal habit. It was only until later when the World Health Organisation came up and announced the dangerous effects of smoking on health. The countries made it mandatory to put signs across the movie theatres, TV programmes and Cigarette packets that smoking is injurious to health and it causes cancer. Many governments made it illegal to sell cigarettes to persons below 18.

Similarly, computer gaming seemed very harmless when it came out in the 90s but as we know the world of gaming has expanded much fold. The hyper-realistic graphics in games make it very addictive to play. The Asians are always one step ahead of the west in terms of everything. Take the example of Japan from sound catching pillows and square watermelons to shoe umbrellas.[104] You can call these inventions crazy cool or absolutely weird. The source of Japan's technological advancement is undoubtedly from the youth of Japan. Statistics show that among 34 OECD countries Japanese students performance levels at first in science and second in maths. Japan spends around 3.59% of GDP on public spending on education.

India too has given many Nobel laureates, CEOs, Scientists to the world Rabindranath Tagore, Mother Teresa and Amartya Sen to name a few. However, when it comes to vices and substance abused Asians don't shy away. In South Korea, video games are big business. Some professional gamers are now so famous that they have become household names and contributed more than 13 trillion won (US$11.2 billion) to the economy last year, according to the Korea Creative Content Agency. I have enjoyed a lot of games growing up as a kid, at that time one could play Counter-Strike. This game was a multiplayer first-person shooter video game in which teams of terrorist battle to perpetrate an act of terror (bombing, hostage-taking, assassination) while counter-terrorists try to prevent it. Back in those days I would sometimes bunk my afternoon tuitions and play this game along with 6-10 friends at a Cyber Cafe nearby. We would sit at the computer sipping chilled coke and try to win as many matches as possible. Hours would go by in front of these computers. Simon who ran the Cyber Cafe there would occasionally remind us of the time "it's 5:30, do you want to play more?" at 5:30 our tuition ended and our parents came to pick us up, ready to go home. I still go

---

[104] '16 CRAZY JAPANESE INVENTIONS THE QUESTIONABLE ART OF CHINDOGU' *Ripley's Believe It or Not!*, May 26, 2017. Retrieved from https://www.ripleys.com/weird-news/chindogu/

to this Cyber Cafe sometimes to get prints and photocopies. It reminds me of my nostalgic times.

Gaming has evolved and now gamers can engage in mobile multiplayer games. PUBG was the hot cake in India. This game allowed you to play with 100 players as opposed to Counter-Strike in which one could only play with 30-35. Call of Duty is also available on smartphones now, earlier it was available only on Xbox, PC and PlayStation. With over 628 million online gamers, India has emerged as one of the top 5 gaming countries. But a recent decision by the World Health Organisation has got some people in the gaming industry worried. In May 2019, the Geneva-based body voted to officially add "gaming disorder" to its International Classification of Diseases, describing it as a pattern of behaviour in which the player has "impaired control" and gives priority to gaming "over other activities to the extent that gaming takes precedence"

Gaming seems like a harmless form of entertainment but online gaming in South Korea has made some teens prone to severe mental health issues. Up to 16 per cent of the country's teens are at risk of developing some kind of gaming addiction, according to Shim Yong-chool, from the National Centre for Youth Internet Addiction Treatment, citing a government survey into internet and smartphone use.

He said most of the young people he helps to treat who "heavily depend on games" tend to exhibit signs of depression and use gaming as an "escape route". Treatment, therefore, focuses more on what is making them depressed, than their addiction to video games. There have been reports in the past of gamers dying after marathon sessions in these Internet cafes!! but for Kim Yong-Gyu, a 20-year-old studying game studies at Sangmyung University "going to PC bangs and playing games is the only hobby that a Korean student can realistically have". Dr. Lee Jae-Won, a neuropsychiatrist at Gangnam Eulji Hospital in Seoul, told Shea that online gaming accounts for roughly 90% of addiction cases in South Korea.

Mr. Lee Kae Seong, the owner of the OZ PC Bang in Seoul's upmarket Gangnam neighbourhood in south Korea while speaking to NPR media said "I've seen a lot of customers come here late in the afternoon and leave the next morning. That's pretty common," says. Some, he says, stay a day or two. And others become…well, ripe. "Some customers who play for too long, I'm sorry to say, they get smelly," he says. "And other customers start to complain. So we have to ask them to leave."[105] People glued to their chair playing video games at a stretch for a day or two may seem rather odd but gaming is so addictive because it works on the same dopamine-principle. Modern games are very sophisticated in terms of graphics, design and storyline. The games have rewards each time you complete a task and these act as a reward each time you complete a mission. In a game, you are presented with game money, weapons, cars etc. which make you happy. The problem is these rewards then are replaced with real-life rewards.

Since a Gamer already receives rewards in games easily after completing the given task at hand he does not feel the need to engage in real-life tasks which are rewarding as these tasks don't give the same amount of happiness or rush.

In late July 2017, a South Korean 21-year-old online-gaming addict was found dead in his home in Inchon, South

---

[105] Michael Sullivan, 'Hooked On The Internet, South Korean Teens Go Into Digital Detox' *npr.org,* August 13, 2019. Retrieved from https://www.npr.org/2019/08/13/748299817/hooked-on-the-internet-south-korean-teens-go-into-digital-detox

Korea.[106] This young boy would play these games intensely after graduating from high school, "he rarely slept or left his room", said his family members. The boy had developed difficulty in breathing; he had complained about this to his family members two months prior but he had refused to see a doctor.

In 2005 a 28-year-old man collapsed and died from organ failure after playing for 50 hours straight. He had apparently just lost his job because of his online gaming habit.[107] Yet in another case, a video game broadcasting company based in South Korea met an unnamed gamer who could be the star of the esports world. In an interview, the boy told the interviewee that he spends 84-88 hours a week gaming! He also added that his life is mostly eating, taking showers, sleeping and being in front of the computer screen. when asked about his future career plans, the boy replied: "I have nothing". Answers like these petrify the Korean government.

I recall as a kid I would play this role-playing game (RPG) called Grand Theft Auto San Andreas for 2-3 hours at a stretch, I was technically hooked on this game which allowed the player to do almost anything like real-life scenarios. RPG games are very common. A young married couple from Suwon submerged themselves in an RPG game where they took care of a virtual baby while their real baby starved to death. The couple was charged with negligent homicide but the wife's sentence was suspended as she was pregnant.

---

[106] Carolyn Sun, 'South Korea's Video Game Addiction' *Newsweek*, 10/17/11. Retrieved from https://www.newsweek.com/south-koreas-video-game-addiction-68309

[107] Ibid.

In South Korea the online game industry is huge. In 2008 it earned \$1.1 billion in exports, according to the Ministry of Culture, which is more than half of the country's entire overseas revenue.[108] This online revenue-generating gaming industry comes at a heavy cost, and it is so severe that online gaming accounts for roughly 90% of addiction cases in the country. One-quarter of teens diagnosed with internet addiction will be hospitalized in a government-sponsored centre. In an interview published by Business Insider with Dr. Lee Jae-Won, a neuropsychiatrist at Gangnam Eulji Hospital said that "The notion of addiction treatment has changed," "For example, the goal of treating someone with a drug addiction problem would be for the person to stop taking drugs completely."[109]

"But for internet addiction treatment, it's not about avoiding using the internet as a whole. It's more about a patient being able to control their use of the internet like a normal person. That is when we can say that they are cured."

Times have changed the meaning of Addiction and has given it a much more horizon. If someone had said twenty years ago that porn addiction is possible we would have turned a blind eye but it is not so in the 21st century. Addiction is not restricted to drugs alone as exemplified from the Korean cases of Game addicts; internet and Mobile-MacBook have made it possible to get addicted to virtual imagery whether it is porn or games.

---

[108] Ibid.

[109] Melia Robinson, 'Korea's internet addiction crisis is getting worse, as teens spend up to 88 hours a week gaming', March 25, 2015. Retrieved from https://www.businessinsider.in/tech/Koreas-internet-addiction-crisis-is-getting-worse-as-teens-spend-up-to-88-hours-a-week-gaming/articleshow/46690833.cms

What's more saddening is that how easily accessible porn is to a 12-year-old unlike cigarette packets most porn websites don't have a warning at least selling cigarettes to children is a crime but there are not enough restrictions on porn. The Korean government has tried to contain the situation of gaming addiction bypassing "Cinderella Act" which prohibits children below 16 years of age to play games but they can easily circumvent and get access to games by giving an I.D of their parents.

The World Health Organization has already officially voted to adopt the latest edition of its International Classification of Diseases, or ICD, to include an entry on "gaming disorder" as a behavioural addiction. The introspecting question that we need to ask is do we wait around till a big organization like WHO comes up with warnings like Porn causes mental health issues similar to online gaming? Do we wait till Governments reach an agreement and flash advertisements on TV channels that Porn reduces grey matter in the brain like they do similar ads for smoking? or are we waiting for this problem to grow severe to such an extent that we have an entire generation of people who have normalized porn addiction and screwed their reward structure and are not able to contribute anything to humanity? In India we already have a porn rehabilitation centre in Gujarat with more individuals at home due to Lockdown during this Pandemic people get bored that is when they are more prone to watch Porn and this crippling addiction will grow into a major mental health issue, it's only a matter of time before more of these Rehab centres are open all across India.

Porn and Criminality

"Pornography is the theory, and rape is the practice."
— Robin Morgan, Feminist

In November 1984 an angry group of women were protesting a pornographic bookstore on Lake Street in Minneapolis.[110] They were part of a national movement of women who rallied under the phrase coined by radical feminist Robin Morgan: Pornography is the theory, and rape is the practice. Andrea Dworkin and Catherine MacKinnon had pioneered Minneapolis and Indianapolis ordinances that define pornography a civil-rights violation against women. Dorkin's radical feminist critique of pornography and violence against women began with her first book, Woman Hating, published in 1974 when she was 27.[111] Dworkin-MacKinnon Anti-

---

[110] Kevin Ehrman-Solberg, "'Pornography is the theory and rape is the practice'" *THE HISTORYPOLIS PROJECT,* March 18, 2014. Retrieved from http://historyapolis.com/blog/2014/03/18/pornography-is-the-theory-and-rape-is-the-practice/

[111] 'Feminist writer and anti-pornography activist Andrea Dworkin dies 2005', *nwmindia.org.* Retrieved from http://www.nwmindia.org/newsmaker/feminist-writer-and-anti-pornography-activist-andrea-dworkin-dies

Pornography Civil Rights Ordinance was most striking because it would have given those directly harmed by pornography a right to civil recourse, enabling the victims to sue porn producers and distributors.[112] However, this ordinance was well received and supported globally it did not see the light. Dworkin continues to inspire anti-porn feminist movements even after her demise.

To many of us nowadays porn is the only source of sex education and when this is the case we ought to ask what syllabus does this teacher use? One of the participants in our Google survey, when asked about why she/he feels sex education is important, said "By Sex Ed, I don't just mean educating kids about sex, but also pleasure and the various ways it can manifest. Healthy ways for its manifestation must be sought. Unhealthy/alarming ways pointed out. It's important to teach kids that their feelings are not wrong or shameful, but the actions arising from those feelings can be."

Another user answered on why he/she thinks sex ed is important: "Like me, many people are actually learning about sex from porn, and no matter how much it is pleasurable to consume porn, I really have to say it's not at all the right way to learn about sex.

Porn doesn't talk about safe sex, consent and many different nuances about sex that are very important. Which is why many people are actually suffering from ignorance.

Thus sex ed is definitely is something we should talk about and take it seriously."

---

[112] Julie Bindel, 'Why Andrea Dworkin is the radical, visionary feminist we need in our terrible times', *The Guardian*, 16 April 2019. Retrieved from https://www.theguardian.com/lifeandstyle/2019/apr/16/why-andrea-dworkin-is-the-radical-visionary-feminist-we-need-in-our-terrible-times

Porn can get pretty brutal. We don't have a mechanism in place which will bifurcate brutal and non-brutal porn. consumers of porn will engage in finding out what turns them on most. Finding your sexual desire is not a vice but one needs guidance and the right mindset. Porn industries make it incredibly difficult to have the right mindset because they believe in no boundaries whatsoever, every click that people make is a profit for these industries. In their quest to search their deepest sexual desires they are more likely to find themselves in a place they don't want to be. In 2012 Natalie Persel who has a PhD in sociology from the University of California did a content analysis where she looked at hundred most popular and best selling porn movies.[113] She found: aggressive, abusive and coercive acts in almost every single movie. The study also showed how the porn since the beginning to now has increasingly become more humiliating she also saw that Ass to mouth, gagging, Double-penetration and choking were included in almost every single movie. Here ass to mouth basically means the penis was inserted in the anus and reached the mouth, gagging meant the penis was inserted in the mouth to an extent that it gave a gagging reflex to the woman, these acts were introduced heavily in porn since the year 2000. Twenty years before that these were basically unheard of.

While analysing the best porn movies of the year 2004-2005 in the United states the random samples were taken from these movies showed that nine out of ten samples showed physical aggression. Out of these five out of ten samples showed verbal aggression like Bitch and slut. Most of the people who were

---

[113] Martin Boeddeke, 'How To Overcome Porn Addiction', *FINDFOCUS*, April 17, 2020. Retrieved from https://findfocus.net/how-to-overcome-porn-addiction/

subjected to this aggression were women and almost every woman reacted to this response is positive or neutral. The response was never negative. In real life imagine if I patted on your cheek your response would be a smile but if I slapped you your response would be defence or retaliate but surprisingly it is completely opposite in porn! You either stay neutral or you either grow or ask for more. Now let's take a pause and let's look at what Norms, What rules and What standards porn has created for Sex.

What is more shocking is whenever there is Sexual offence committed in India like rape the videos of such crimes are searched on popular Porn websites.[114] The Kathua Rape in which a child was raped brutally and killed was a top search in Porn Website called Xvideos similarly Google trends showed that when a Doctor from Andhra Pradesh was raped by truck drivers the videos of the incidents were top searches when the news of the incident surfaced Media such incidents remind us of how pervasive society we live in.

American feminist and professor of law, Catharine Alice MacKinnon whose work primarily took aim at sexual abuse in the context of inequality.[115] MacKinnon, whose work has helped shape thinking about harassment, goes on to say that "there is no moral difference between really degrading pornography and the concentration camp videos" she thinks "freedom of speech" allows the stronger, more dominant

---

[114] Prasenjeet Dhage, 'Female Liberation: Understanding the magnitude of sexual violence against women' *Goa News Hub*, December 9, 2019. Retrieved from https://goanewshub.com/female-liberation-understanding-the-magnitude-of-sexual-violence-against-women/

[115] 'Catharine A. MacKinnon American feminist and law professor', *Britannica.* Retrieved from https://www.britannica.com/biography/Catharine-A-MacKinnon

speaker to silence the weaker ones, and believes that women have been silenced by the speech of men.[116] Women are the worst sufferers of pornography because through porn they are just reduced to some of their body parts. There are laws which protect women against sexual harassment at the workplace but what about when they are not at work? What about the videos that normalise sexual abuse?

It is a popular notion that pornography influences the behaviour of Indian men more than in other cultures. Trans-cultural variations are described as a common reason. In India, any discussion about sex is considered "taboo," and most people do not have even basic sex education. Sex education provides factual information about sexuality, which counteracts the messages about sexuality presented in pornography. Without adequate sex education, it is suggested that pornography would serve to act as a "permission-giving" agency by promoting wrong notions about the sexuality of women and children, thus breeding sexual violence.

Mainstream, popular pornography websites consistently feature videos that promote sexual violence and violence, more often against women. These videos depict giving preference to men's orgasm and sexual pleasure than women.

Many of these videos specifically and intentionally promote violent themes including incest; fathers and stepfathers raping their children; groups of men raping unwitting female victims; abduction and rape; and tricking women into sex by lying to them. Mainstream porn also normalizes and promotes extremely violent behaviours like strangulation; forcing a woman to gag on an object or during oral sex; simultaneously

---

[116] 'Mackinnon: Pornography is Oppression', *spectacle.org*. Retrieved from http://www.spectacle.org/1195/mack.html

forcing penises or objects into women's mouths, vaginas, and rectums; and humiliating, belittling, and yelling at women.

Mainstream, popular porn also regularly depicts the following scenarios: women always wanting sex; women saying "no" and initially resisting sex, but eventually changing their minds and enjoying forced sex; and women enjoying humiliating situations, strangulation, and other physical assaults.

Using a wide range of methodologies, researchers from several disciplines have shown that viewing pornography is associated with damaging outcomes.[117] In a study of U.S. college men, researchers found that 83 percent reported seeing mainstream pornography, and from these those who believed that "they wouldn't be caught", were more likely to say they would commit rape or sexual assault than men who hadn't seen porn in the past 12 months. Porn routinely promotes characteristics of hostile masculinity, which show men being angry at women and seeking revenge through sex. Pornography also frequently promotes patriarchal gender norms, that men need to be aggressive and dominant, while women need to be submissive and compliant. hence it is no surprise that in the same study it was found that porn consumers were less likely to intervene if they observed a sexual assault taking place. It seems likely that if men consistently receive these messages about lack of empathy and absence of connections which in turn teach men and women how they are supposed to behave, they will be influenced by these messages in some way. Hence, Pornography can be correlated with sexual violence and murder.

---

[117] Gail Dines, 'Is porn immoral? That doesn't matter: It's a public health crisis.', *The Washington Post*, April 8, 2016. Retrieved from https://www.washingtonpost.com/posteverything/wp/2016/04/08/is-porn-immoral-that-doesnt-matter-its-a-public-health-crisis/

Sexual violence is connected to many other things as well and vice versa, just like high religiosity (not spiritualism) is related to violence look at the crusades as an example, especially when we consider the number of individuals currently using porn.

Watching even nonviolent pornography is correlated with the consumer being more likely to use verbal coercion, drugs, and alcohol to push women into sex. Psychologists also argue that porn depicts culturally accepted standards of beauty they also propagate the myth that men and women have insatiable sexual appetites.[118] An analysis of 33 different studies found that exposure to both non-violent and violent porn increases aggressive behaviour, including having violent fantasies and even actually committing violent assaults. Still, consider how it's no surprise then that people who already have violent tendencies are perhaps more affected by pornography. Of course, I am not claiming that pornography automatically turns people into kidnapping rapists, because the reality is that probably 99.9% of the people who look at pornography are everyday people with regular every day lives, people who are not going to go out and commit a crime because of what they watch online.

However, as research and current events are showing, there is a common behaviour among people who commit heinous crimes–they often have an unusually high interest in porn and usually have a long history with it that typically extends back to their childhood.

The Majority of porn i.e. violent as well as non-violent portrays men and women differently. Men are projected

---

[118] Sam Carr, 'How pornography removes empathy – and fosters harassment and abuse', *THE CONVERSATION,* November 2, 2017. Retrieved from https://theconversation.com/how-pornography-removes-empathy-and-fosters-harassment-and-abuse-86643

as aggressive, dominant and even abusive while women as submissive and obedient even during abuse. This sets an agenda for future relationships that a person has, Normalizing verbal as well as non-verbal abuse this leads to change into a toxic attitude toward one another in a relationship. Watching aggressive porn directly leads to aggressive behaviour detrimental to both the abuser and the victim.

In 2016, a team of leading researchers did A Meta-Analysis of Pornography Consumption and Actual Acts of Sexual Aggression in General Population Studies published in Journal of Communication in which they compiled all the research they could find on the subject. After examining twenty-two studies they concluded that the research left, "little doubt that, on the average, individuals who consume pornography more frequently are more likely to hold attitudes conducive [favourable] to sexual aggression and engage in actual acts of sexual aggression."[119]

Our brains have what scientists call "mirror neurons"—rain cells that fire not only when we do things ourselves, but also when we watch other people do things, in a movie theatre the audience will try to dodge a punch in response to a movie which involves a lot of action like "Rocky", some movies come in 3D this enhances the experience even more. This is because we have developed involuntary reflexes this is also why movies can make

---

[119] 'How Consuming Porn Can Lead To Violence, It's no secret that much of porn is violent, but many people don't understand the extent to which porn's underlying messages influence behavior. Porn is full of people, particularly women, being disrespected, coerced, and physically and verbally abused, and that's shaping how society thinks and acts.' *fightthenewdrug.org*, August 23, 2017. Retrieved from https://fightthenewdrug.org/how-consuming-porn-can-lead-to-violence/

us cry or feel angry or scared.[120] Essentially, mirror neurons let us share the emotion of other people's experiences as we watch. These neurons are active when we learn new motor skills as well as when we see others doing an action. So when a person is looking at porn, he or she naturally starts to respond to the emotions of the actors seen on the screen. As the consumer becomes aroused, his or her brain gets to work wiring together those feelings of arousal to what is seen happening on the screen, almost as if he or she was actually having the experience. So if a person feels aroused watching a man or woman get kicked around and called names, that individual's brain learns to associate that kind of violence with sexual arousal.

Consumers of porn will claim that they are self-aware when watching porn and do not subscribe to the violence and abuse however the research proves otherwise, it makes consumers believe that women secretly enjoy being raped and to actually be sexually aggressive in real life because porn makes the consumer believe that violence is sexy and acceptable and women enjoy being hurt. The aggression can take the form of verbally harassing or pressuring someone for sex, emotionally manipulating them, threatening to end the relationship unless they grant favours, deceiving them or lying to them about sex, or even physically assaulting them.

Take the example of the doctor who was brutally raped in Hyderabad. On 29th November 2019 when a charred body of a woman was found near a sewage pipeline in Hyderabad who was brutally gang-raped by 4 men the "Hyderabad gang rape video" was searched on google and various Porn websites

---

[120] Sanden Totten, 'New research explains why movies make us feel strong emotions', *scpr.org*, December 4, 2014. Retrieved from https://www. scpr.org/news/2014/12/04/48457/what-watching-movies-can-tell-us-about-how-our-bra/

at an alarming rate however this is not a first time, After the monstrous rape and murder of an eight-year-old girl in Kathua in Jammu and Kashmir, her name, photos and rape video were also the top searches on Google and pornographic websites!

According to Leslee Ludwin the director of India's Daughter who led a 2-year investigation into understanding why men rape, her report is an eye-opener. When she met the convicts of Nirbhya Indian women who was gang-raped in a moving bus and later murdered the media had prepared her to find monsters in the prison and make her think that these are the few rotten apples who needed to be punished as they have committed rape a heinous crime but in her quest in understanding these men she found that it is the barrel that was rotten which made these apples to rot and it is us(society) which teach these men how to think which in turn led them into committing this heinous crime. What's more shocking if not eye-opening is that these men(one of them being a juvenile) did not feel guilty that they have committed any offence. These are incidences make us think that how society has normalized violence against women through Pornography and changed the way we perceive women. Not surprisingly, the more violent the porn they consume, the more likely they will be to support violence and act out violently. In fact, one study found that those with higher exposure to violent porn were six times more likely to have raped someone than those who had low past exposure.

The crimes Ted Bundy is known for today may connect with a deep, dark porn past. Ted Bundy was a notorious American criminal known to have killed at least 36 women in the 1970s.[121] Where does this shocking information come from?

---

[121] Biography.com Editors, 'Ted Bundy Biography', *The Biography.com website,* April 6, 2020. Retrieved from https://www.biography.com/crime-figure/ted-bundy

In the last interview he gave before he was executed on an electric chair, he talked extensively about the impact porn had on him in his formative years and how he became desensitized to the objectification and abuse of women early on.[122] Here's what he said in an interview:

"The most damaging kinds of pornography are those that involve violence and sexual violence," "My experience with pornography that deals on a violent level with sexuality are that once you become addicted to it – and I look at this as a kind of addiction – like other kinds of addiction…I would keep looking for more potent, more explicit, more graphic kinds of materials."[123]

"Like an addiction, you keep craving something which is harder, harder. Something which gives you a greater sense of excitement. Until you reach the point where the pornography only goes so far."[124]

Another challenge that we face is Deepfakes. A Deepfake is a software in which the machine learns to fabricate events

---

[122] 'Porn Didn't Make Ted Bundy A Serial Killer, But That Doesn't Make It Harmless' MAY 3, 2019, *fightthenewdrug.org*. Retrieved from https://fightthenewdrug.org/did-porn-impact-ted-bundy-serial-killer/

[123] Dominic Smithers, 'In His Final Interview Serial Killer Ted Bundy Said Pornography Drove Him To Murder', *LadBible*, 13 December 2018. Retrieved from https://www.ladbible.com/news/news-serial-killer-ted-bundys-final-chilling-interview-20181213#:~:text=News-,In%20His%20Final%20Interview%20Serial%20Killer%20Ted,Pornography%20Drove%20Him%20To%20Murder&text=He%20said%3A%20%22My%20experience%20with,other%20kinds%20of%20addiction…

[124] Ibid.

that never happened.[125] Remember the face swap feature on Snapchat and Instagram where not only the face of your friends but also all the features are swapped. This is how Deepfake works, this is more advanced and anyone's face can be swapped onto another person and the viewer will not be able to tell the difference if it's fake or real. This is a pressing danger we face because this technology can be easily used to manipulate videos.

In a September 2019 survey, Deeptrace revealed that of all the deep fakes videos which had surfaced on the internet they, 96% of them were pornographic. These were mostly women and the face was used without obtaining any consent.[126]

Deepfakes requires hundreds of images to process and learn about the feature of a particular face so that it can be used in a video hence celebrities are the most targeted victims since they have many photos on different websites and movies. With the explosion of social media, it's not only celebrities anymore but also avid social media users who upload their selfies frequently.

Deepfake name originated on a Reddit discussion platform, which talked about swapping celebrity images with a pornstar. Reddit banned the page but the conversion moved to other websites. there is a growing concern because a large number of porn users are ready to pay for videos of their favourite celebrity or someone who they know from Deepfake porn

---

[125] Rob Toews, 'Deepfakes Are Going To Wreak Havoc On Society. We Are Not Prepared.', *Forbes,* May 25, 2020. Retrieved From https://www.forbes.com/sites/robtoews/2020/05/25/deepfakes-are-going-to-wreak-havoc-on-society-we-are-not-prepared/#5931c5bd7494

[126] Ian Sample, 'AI-generated fake videos are becoming more common (and convincing). Here's why we should be worried', *The Guardian,* 13 January 2020. Retrieved from https://www.theguardian.com/technology/2020/jan/13/what-are-deepfakes-and-how-can-you-spot-them

video makers. A Buzzfeed News report by Charlie Warzel said that Pornhub has banned Deepfake celebrity sex videos, but the site is full of them what's more? Pornhub's algorithms not only featured these videos but also promoted this nonconsensual content![127]

---

[127] Charlie Warzel, 'Pornhub Banned Deepfake Celebrity Sex Videos, But The Site Is Still Full Of Them', *BuzzFeed.News,* April 18, 2018. Retrieved from https://www.buzzfeednews.com/article/charliewarzel/ pornhub-banned-deepfake-celebrity-sex-videos-but-the-site

Juvenile Delinquents

The habitual committing of criminal acts or offences by a young person, especially one below the age of 18 are classified as juvenile delinquents.[128] This is a separate category under Criminal psychology and Criminal Penal Code because although juveniles commit a crime they cannot be treated at par with adult criminals as they do not have mental maturity.

The eminent Belgian social statistician observed that adolescents, particularly the young males are prone to crime, disorder and delinquency because of their childish impulsiveness or adolescent conflict.

"The propensity to crime is at its maximum at the age when strength and passions have reached their height, yet when reason has not acquired sufficient control to master their combined influence"
– Adolphe Quetelet, Belgian Social Statistician.

Radzinowicz mentioned in his book "The growth of crime" that neglected children and juveniles fall easy prey to criminality. He asserted that the adolescents claim the highest share in violence

---

[128] Pg. 484 Criminology And Penology by Dr. N.V. Pranjape, 12th edition

due to dashing nature, lack of foresight, uncritical enthusiasm, physical strength, endurance and a desire for adventure.

Since a nation's future depends upon the young generation, children deserve compassion and bestowal of the best care to protect this burgeoning human resource. A child is born innocent and if nourished with tender care and attention, he or she will blossom as a person of stature and excellence. On the other hand obnoxious surroundings, neglect of basic needs, poverty, child abuse and temptations would spoil the child and likely turn him into a delinquent.

It must be acknowledged that the overflowing criminality of youth cannot be attributed to biophysical factors alone. There are other factors which sway the criminality in youth such as a change in social, economical and political change, pattern of education, Population explosion and media. Among these under the pattern of education, sex education is an important chapter which is neglected in India, Sex education can be defined as programs offering information on sexuality and contraception. This also encompasses the gender identity, consent and awareness about sexual abuse. It aims to develop an awareness of sexual health. It also includes exploring values and beliefs about topics related to sexuality and gaining the skills that are needed to navigate relationships and manage one's own sexual health.[129] Circumventing this program in our education system is proving to be responsible for the sexual offences against male as well as female.

In a survey conducted by us, it was found that 53% of participants found Pornography at the age of 13-16 while 14% found it at the age of 6-12!

---

[129] 'What is Sex Education?', *Planned Parenthood.* Retrieved from https:// www.plannedparenthood.org/learn/for-educators/what-sex-education

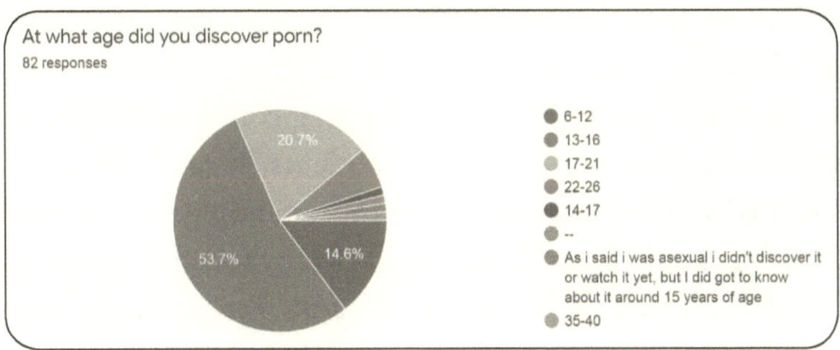

Any discussion over 'sex' education continues to be elusive in India.[130] It is not only met with boundless shilly-shallying but not to mention it is also believed that education about sexuality is a private matter, it goes against Indian culture or leads to immorality and promiscuity amongst adolescents.

In India, almost all children will receive sex education through Pornography. when as the child hits puberty he has hormonal changes in his body which cause him and her go through different biological and mental changes the children aged 12-18 have an impulse to be rebellious, sadly enough this impulse is understood in a wrong light and in school as well as family and friends sex education, sexuality and bodily changes is something which is not talked about. rather some children are ridiculed at this tender age for their bodily changes leaving a deep dark psychological mark on the students.

The term 'sex' and 'sexuality' carries a lot of taboo within the premise of the school especially in presence of authority. In most schools, there is a complete lack of proper dialogue

---

[130] The Bastion Staff, 'A Missed Opportunity: Addressing Sexuality Education in the Draft NEP' *THE BASTION*, July 31, 2019. Retrieved from https://thebastion.co.in/politics-and/education/a-missed-opportunity-addressing-sexuality-education-in-the-draft-nep/

around sexuality education. Even if there are certain attempts of initiating conversations, it did not cross the line beyond menstrual hygiene. Even if there is a conversation around sexuality between teachers and students, it takes place very informally. My first exposure to understanding sex was when I was 14 yrs old me and my friends were excited at the bodily changes happening in our body and were curious about subjects like masturbation, sex, orgasm. A memory disk filled with porn would be circulated among the boys little did I and my friends know that this was something which would prove detrimental to us as well as our relations with different people. Perhaps if we weren't so consumed with guilt and shame about sexuality these porn movies wouldn't carry the weight they do now but then we wouldn't be interested in these films either. If the fruit were not forbidden would anyone care to take a bite? Could it be that the porn industry has taken advantage of this guilt and shame hence its a booming business?

Eating the forbidden apple is the majority case with Indian highschool going students who have no knowledge about their body. Children are curious about sex and sexuality as there is always a sense of 'quietness' about such matters. Dr. Sigmund Freud, a renowned psychiatrist of 19th century Europe suggests that it creates within them a fundamental conflict which he calls the 'ideals of education'. Children want to know about sexuality, but their parents and teachers tell them they need to know about something else.[131]

---

[131] By Joyoti Chowdhury, 'Why Is Sex Or Sexuality Education In Indian Schools Still A Taboo?', *Feminism in India,* March 9, 2020. Retrieved from https://feminisminindia.com/2020/03/09/why-sex-sexuality-education-indian-schools-taboo/

When the inmates of the Delhi prison were asked if they asked for "consent", most of them couldn't answer because they did not know what it meant. Their stories also highlighted a sense of entitlement and ownership over the victim.[132] This behaviour is built up partly because of societal norms and lack of education. Differences of gender intensify during puberty, it is when boys realise how they are different from girls and enjoy certain privileges which are only reserved for them such as autonomy, individuality and power. This leads to misdirected masculinity showing male dominance over females. This further leads to sexual exploitation if men do not educate themselves about sexuality.

Despite the current growing awareness around child sexual abuse, there are still very little attempts taken by schools to incorporate the understanding of the difference between the non-sexual and sexual touch. A study conducted by the Indian Ministry of Women and Child Development and carried out by UNICEF and Prayas, a non-governmental organization provides us insight about these issues. They interviewed 12,247 children and 2324 young adults in 13 Indian states. The study revealed that a shocking 53% of children between the ages of 5 and 12 have been sexually abused. Most often, this abuse was inflicted by parents, legal guardians or close members of the family. Furthermore, the study disturbingly notes that more than half of all these cases of sexual abuse and rape go unreported.[133] Children must be taught the difference

---

[132] Madhumita Pandey, 'How to tackle India's sexual violence epidemic – it starts with sex education' *THE CONVERSATION*, May 15, 2019. Retrieved from https://theconversation.com/how-to-tackle-indias-sexual-violence-epidemic-it-starts-with-sex-education-114381

[133] Ibid.

between a good touch and a bad touch not only for their own safety but also for the safety of other children.[134] A child may touch another child on the private parts without even realising that it is inappropriate. This can be easily avoided with education.

Adolescents aged 10-19 years constitute 325 million of the population, which is one-fourth of the total population.[135] The government of India initiated the 'Adolescent Education Program' (AEP) in 2007 in collaboration with the National AIDS Control Organization (NACO) and the United Nations Children's Fund (UNICEF). The topics of 'attraction' and "Consent" are still left out of these programs.[136] A deep-rooted morality binds the sentiment of Indian society from incorporating sex ed which will teach students about sexuality in a broad sense.

What's more saddening is that although sexual offences are on the rise in India and the Draft National National Education Policy has made no provisions for proper Sex Education. It neither finds mention of that word 'sexuality' nor finds any mention in the document, 'sex education' has been reduced under the component of "Ethical and moral reasoning". Hence It is no surprise that an International Organization 'Youth Coalition for Sexual and Reproductive Rights' said, 'In

---

[134] Natasha Daniels, '10 Ways to Teach Your Child the Skills to Prevent Sexual Abuse', *Child Mind Institute*. Retrieved from https://childmind.org/article/10-ways-to-teach-your-child-the-skills-to-prevent-sexual-abuse/

[135] *NATIONAL AIDS CONTROL ORGANISATION*. Retrieved from http://naco.gov.in/sites/default/files/REPORT%20OF%20THE%20WORKING%20SUB-GROUP%20ON%20ADOLESCENTS%20%26%20YOUTH%20FOR%20NACP-IV.pdf

[136] Ibid.https://feminisminindia.com/2020/03/09/why-sex-sexuality-education-indian-schools-taboo/

India, most schools, private and public affiliated state boards of secondary education don't have any form of sexuality education in their curriculum.

There are a couple of concerns here. One, the focus seemingly continues to be on the nationally and socially serviceable bodies of adolescents – grounded within the continued population and disease control discourses of the pre-and post-Adolescence Education Programme (AEP) decades. Such a medico-legal view of 'sex education' is limiting and myopic. Two, the idea of enabling students to make "future judgement" is unjustifiable. It is understood that early marriages or young people's romantic consensual sexual partnerships require them to build skills much early on to negotiate safe, healthy, and equitable relationships. This group is at an increased risk of sexual and gender-based violence, STDs, unsafe abortions, and teenage pregnancies. In February 2020 the government released a curriculum 'Health and Wellness Curriculum' which talks about teaches students about adolescent health yet the entire syllabus doesn't mention the phrase "sex education". What is needed is A comprehensive curriculum-based sexuality module, such as the one launched by UNESCO in 2018 which can help young boys and girls understand their bodies and the age-related changes better. And it can also teach young people about consent and respecting each others' personal space.

A government-supported study on child sexual abuse in 2007 by the Ministry of Women and Child Development has brought before us some disturbing numbers. 12,447 children and adolescents were interviewed from different 13 states of which 53% reported facing one or more form of sexual abuse, Among these 50% children admitted to having been molested by a person who was trustworthy and close to them. Out of these, 52.94% were boys and 46% girls.[137]

Sex-related crime stem from gender inequality these can be tackled by making young adults understand their bodies better by explaining the concept of consent and boundaries. else the children will be drawn towards pornography and learn about sex which will involve unrealistic imagery, could this mean children will be more prone to sexual attacks if they see extreme sexual imagery? This situation of porn and juvenile delinquency can be greatly exemplified by understanding how sex crimes have increased in the United Kingdom.[138]

Violent porn has increased child on child assault by 400% in the United Kingdom. Statistics published by the UK's Ministry of Justice revealed that since 2011 there was a 74% rise, in convictions of Juveniles and as many as120 children were convicted of rape in 2015. Of the 120 children convicted of rape, 46 were sentenced to detention and 61 received community orders.

A report by the daily mail also said that after watching explicit images online, an 11-year-old boy admitted of committing seven counts of rape and sexual assaults on boys under 13. Magistrates involved in this legal issue joined that this was clearly a case of porn fueled sexual assault. If you are concerned about rape culture and sexual violence, it is

---

[137] Ibid   https://thebastion.co.in/politics-and/education/a-missed-opportunity-addressing-sexuality-education-in-the-draft-nep/

[138] Ian Drury, 'Extreme internet porn is fuelling a surge in sex attacks by children: Number of under-17s convicted of rape almost doubles in four years', *Daily Mail,* 13 February 2017. Retrieved from https://www.dailymail.co.uk/news/article-4217768/Extreme-porn-fuelling-surge-sex-attacks-children.html#ixzz4YWbUr6eT

important to ask yourself this question: Even if pornography is just a fantasy and a form of harmless entertainment, why do we think it is acceptable for men to fantasize about and be entertained by violence against women?

How Cultures Have Suppressed Sex

Indian families and by extension, society, has become proficient in dismissal and living in the shadow of denial especially when it comes to those important conversations about sex. In an online survey by Team Dopamine trap, we found that 67% of applicants' family did not discuss the bodily changes that they went through during puberty.

It is often for societies and families to come to terms with the fact that their girls are sexually active after a certain age and are free to make their own decisions. Despite living in the modern time our generation continues to face the brunt of long-entrenched stigmas and social taboos associated with topics like sex which has, in turn, led to a complete break down in communication, especially at home with our families.

Sex ed was not taboo at all in ancient India if truth to be told ancient society was very liberal towards the discussion of sex and the human body. Some of the things mentioned in Kamasutra which were written between 400 BCE and 300 CE would be outrageous to many even by today's liberal standards. Most people believe Kamasutra is about different sex positions but there is more to it than meets the eye. For instance, sex positions are forbidden if women are down with a fever, pregnant, extremely corpulent, lately delivered or deformed. Use of any position in these cases is forbidden because of the possibility of very bad after-effects. Vatsyayana also mentions homosexual women who indulge in sexual practices with the help of artificial aids.[139] Kamasutra talks about not only how to begin sex but also gives systematic end. According to Sutras 13-22: after sex, the gratified lovers need to wash and have plenty of water. This will be followed by the consumption of mixed vegetables, juices, citron, meat and mutton soup. Sex makes people lose bodily fluids, the average women burn 70 calories while men burn 100, this could be more if you have read about different positions in Kamasutra and/or your partners' athleticism. Hence eating good food will help your body revitalize better.[140]

Coming back to India, Somehow conversations about sex have always been confined to the risks of teenage pregnancy and transmission of STDs as we talked in the last chapter rather than the emotional toll that sexual and physical relationships can have on us as well as the impacts and discovery of female desire and pleasure.[141] Remember that time As kids when a hot and heavy scene comes in a movie the kids will awkwardly look away in front of their parents. fast forward to adulthood female pleasure and independence is mostly ignored, the only purpose of sex for a woman is thought to be procreation, setting up a family and taking care of her husband.

---

[139] S. C. Upadhyaya, *Kama Sutra of Vatsyayana*, First edition, 1961.

[140] Ibid.

[141] Shivani Ekkanath, 'It's 2020! Why Are We Still So Afraid To Talk About Sex And Sexuality? By Shivani Ekkanath', *Feminism in India,* February 6, 2020. Retrieved From https://feminisminindia. com/2020/02/06/2020-still-so-afraid-talk-sex-sexuality/

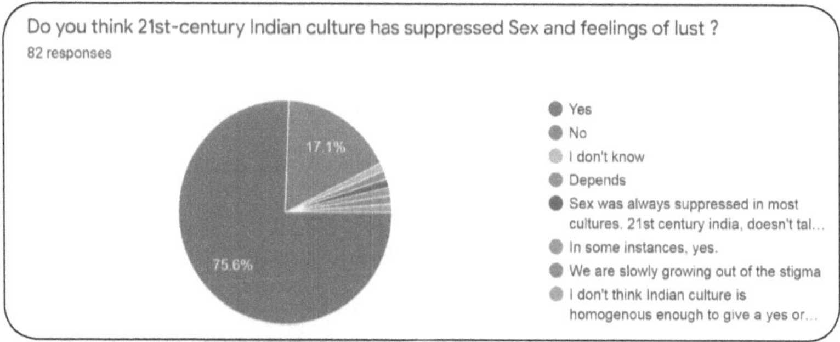

75% of people in our survey think that 21st-century Indian culture has suppressed sex and feelings of lust. For some people, sexy thoughts bring up excitement and anticipation around past sexual encounters or possible future experiences. Lingering on these thoughts might turn you on or lead to masturbation which is totally normal but If you're dealing with sexual repression, even the word "sex" could trigger embarrassment or shame. Unfortunately, this is the case in the majority of the Indian families masturbation is looked down upon and is often treated as immoral the irony being that psychiatrists say if you don't masturbate it would be abnormal. The topic of Sex is seldom discussed, Indian parents believe this is something that naturally comes to ones understanding with – age.

Psychologists say family is one of the groups which has a major influence on a child as the child grows up. Family views will have a major impact on what the child's beliefs as this is the reason many children born and brought up in a family which supports right-wing politics or left-wing political will have more inclination towards those ideologies. Of course, there are few exceptions but this case of the child adopting the views of the parents is in majority.

When topics like sex are off-limits at the family dinner table and are looked down upon, the child automatically associates these with negative thoughts. Especially during the puberty stage when discussing the bodily changes and sex becomes crucial because the child has natural sexual impulse and curiosity about the human body. How an act which gives rise to procreation and a complete human being (when the sperm fertilizes the egg) can be looked down upon and turned a blind eye to is still a mystery to me. Perhaps succeeding generations of human beings have associated sex, Orgasm and feelings of lust with Vice. Mother nature never makes mistakes, these emotions exist in us for a reason, understanding these emotions will help us channelize them better. The constant denial the modern culture built around this taboo of turning a blind eye towards sex has given rise to the perversion of which the Porn Industries heavily take advantage. According to Huffington Post, May 2013 "Porn sites get more visitors each month than Netflix, Amazon and Twitter combined". When a boy becomes a man Porn has become the Sex ed. for him especially when 90% of the Porn contains at least one aggressive act verbal or physical or both it is teaching young boys that it is okay to be violent towards women during sex. Almost one-third of the internet consists of Pornography in some form or the other, Boys and Girls who are growing up in this increasingly hypersexualized Pop culture which normalises violence and teaches young girls to fuck or be invisible.

The mainstream porn showcasing toxic masculinity is made by men for men it won't be wrong to say that it is outright misogynistic. Keeping addictions aside have you ever wondered why can't porn be made for entertainment and pleasure for women. I mean it can still be explicit and treat women as human beings rather than seeing them merely as objects of pleasure for men. What will the woman get in return for giving a passionate head to her partner, will the man focus on what she likes? Sex requires two individuals and should be a pleasurable experience for both. Sexual pleasure is not only taboo in a patriarchal society but also in pornography. This is where feminist pornography or ethical pornography comes in. Which provides a pleasurable experience for not only men but also women.[142] Ethical porn focuses on the welfare of the performer, respecting their boundaries and it encourages women in their pursuit of freedom through sexuality, equality, and pleasure.[143] However mainstream porn consumers have become desensitized to violence because mainstream porn is free and offers extreme acts which are normalised and sold as ways to pursue pleasure this is why ethical porn does not grow as much as its counterpart.

Unlike pornography, dating apps offer real intimate relationships. One would think it should be okay to find dates in these apps. Looking for love can be good Especially, with avid social media users who are looking for a casual relationship, life partner or just fornication. However, Indians seem to be secretly approving of porn but not dating apps and websites. Young Indian women are terrified if their parents find out if they are swiping left or right on Tinder app which is ironic because India is the largest market for Tinder in Asia which means Indians are broadening their horizons in the dating world. For most women than men this horizon needs to be explored discreetly because if society comes to know, what will

---

[142] Dyuti Gupta, 'Can Feminist Porn Give Women The Equal Right To Pleasure And Satisfaction?' *shethepeole*, June 26, 2020. Retrieved from https://www.shethepeople.tv/top-stories/opinion/feminist-porn-equal-right-satisfaction/

[143] Amanda Chatel, 'Ethical Porn That Focuses On Female Pleasure', *Bustle*, Aug. 6, 2020. Retrieved from https://www.bustle.com/wellness/places-watch-ethical-porn-female-pleasure

they think? It is unacceptable for Indian society to acknowledge that a woman is sexually active even if she is not married.

"There needs to be a critical appraisal of the status of women in India," said Sunil Yawlikar who is an artist, writer and a poet based in Maharashtra. "Female sexuality was repressed since ancient India with the advent of Aryans who wanted to establish their dominance." "Since 50% of humans are females they introduced patriarchy which undermined the sexuality of women, this way they could dominate half of the humans." Wendy O'Flaherty who holds a D. Phil. degree in 'Oriental Studies' from Oxford University, with a dissertation on The Origins of Heresy in Hindu Mythology has similar views. She has characterized the Rig Veda, the earliest collection of Aryan religious hymns dating from about 1000 to 800 B.C., as "a book by men about male concerns in a world dominated by men [and] one of these concerns is women…" O'Flaherty then divides the hymns about women into conversation hymns and marriage hymns. Both types are concerned with the sexual rejection of the female by the male.[144]

During the reign of Mughal dynasty emperor, Akbar made a rule that the daughters of the dynasty would not marry. As a result girls of the Mughal dynasty have illegally resorted to courtiers and relatives who would use them to quench their sexual thirst. Historians often blam Shah Jahan for being infamous for his sexuality. Historian Francis Vernier wrote that Shah Jahan and Mumtaz Mahal's elder daughter Jahanara looked exactly like her mother. This is why he was sexually active with her by manipulation after the demise

---

[144] Sarla R. Murgai, 'Ramusack, Barbara. "WOMEN IN SOUTH AND SOUTHEAST ASIA" Introduction to South Asia', *University of Tennessee at Chattanooga.* Retrieved from https://www.utc.edu/faculty/ sarla-murgai/women-in-south-asia.php

of Mumtaz.[145] Mughal daughters were also forbidden from having a lover who was a non-muslim. Jahanara Begum had a lover who was a commoner, this was unacceptable to Shaha Jahan. When he heard of this affair he reached the palace of Jahanara unannounced. Jahanara who was caught in a frenzy of fear hid her lover in a cauldron used for baths. This is when the emperor ordered the servants to light the fire under the cauldron "for the princess' bath" and boiled the lover to a bloody death.[146]

Commenting on how mythologies associate serpent with phallus Sunil reckons "It's no coincidence that serpent is associated with male phallus because Sigmund Freud the founder of psychoanalysis also believed that snakes were connected to sex so also our libido." In some Indian culture for instance king Cobra symbolises masculine energy. Freud opined that snake dreams were connected to "male reproductive organ" and that a person's dreams were in turn connected to their subconscious mind. Sunil depicts the freedom of sexuality among men and women in art, the former being sexually liberated while the latter being the opposite.

---

[145] News Crab, 'Shah Jahan was the most lustful emperor in Mughal history! Had a relationship with daughter, after the death of his wife' 22 May, *dailyhunt*. Retrieved from https://m.dailyhunt.in/news/india/english/news+crab-epaper-newcrb/shah+jahan+was+the+most+lustful+emperor+in+mughal+history+had+a+relationship+with+daughter+after+the+death+of+his+wife-newsid-n186287316

[146] Syed Mubin Zehra, 'Female desire in the Mughal dynasty: Daughters broke chastity norms, but had limited agency, Little is written about the Mughal daughters' sexuality in texts representative of that period, but foreigners' travelogues and contemporary literature tell us about their affairs and the fate of their lovers', *Firstpost.*, December 13, 2018. Retrieved from https://www.firstpost.com/india/female-desire-in-the-mughal-dynasty-daughters-broke-chastity-norms-but-had-limited-agency-5695341.html

Not only Indian aunties who'd judge you for your every breath but also Indian men who have no chill when it comes to dating on Tinder. According to Pratika Yashaswi who interviewed dating app users in Huffington post, she talked to a young girl from Kolkata Anamika who is 21 years old, Kolkata-based fashion-communications student, she says "Just the fact that I'm on a dating app is enough for my DMs to be flooded with dick pics and derogatory messages," "If I have to put [an interest in hook-ups] in my Tinder bio, I have to phrase it in a way that doesn't make me look easy. Otherwise, guys get cocky. They believe that just because you're interested in casual sex, you're going to be interested in them so they don't put in the effort." The misguided masculinity coupled with lack of sex education shows up in ugly ways and dismissive attitudes of Indian society towards sex makes it worse. This also puts women in a situation wherein they have to face a lot of disrespect in the streets as well as in sheets.[147]

---

[147] Pratika Yashaswi, 'Indian Women Are Swiping Right For Casual Sex, But Are They Getting It? Hooking up is a battle when you can't switch off cultural sanctions and anxieties.', *HUFFPOST*, 16 February 2020. Retrieved from https://www.huffingtonpost.in/entry/indian-women-are-swiping-right-for-casual-sex-but-are-they-getting-it_in_5e47c877c5b64ba2974ffa96

LGBTQ+ & Porn

Studies have addressed pornography through the lenses of addiction, misogyny, sexual exploration, and sexual liberation but these are from the heteronormative perspective if we have to understand this subject deeper we have to see how all humans react to pornography and how it affects everyone including LGBTQ+ community. People find it easy to accept that t clothing, language, and music are cultural, invented, created, and possibly alterable but often find it difficult to accept that gender and sexuality are not the same but are greatly influenced by culture.

Sexuality and gender are much like food. We eat to survive at the same time we can enjoy what we eat. The meaning of what constitutes "delicious" or "repulsive" is also set by the culture.[148] For instance, Indian food being spicy many Europeans find it repulsive because they are culturally used to

---

[148] Carol C. Mukhopadhyay, San Jose State University, Tami Blumenfield, Furman University with Susan Harper, Texas Woman's University and Abby Gondek, 'Perspectives: An Open Invitation to Cultural Anthropology', "Gender and Sexuality", *OER Services.* Retrieved from https://courses.lumenlearning.com/suny-culturalanthropology/chapter/gender_and_sexuality/

a different type of food. Many potential edible items are not food eg. cat, dog and honeybee in India. Similarly, a dessert after food, a romantic dinner or a prasad from the temple is a complex cultural invention. So gender and sexuality just like eating are biological components but with the advance of culture, we have created different meanings around these which continue to govern us.[149] Researchers believe that sexuality can be fluid for some individuals, for most people, however, sexual orientation is stable and unchanging. More women are more likely to have fluid sexuality than men.

Today we have a definite distinction in gender which is male, female, lesbian, gay, bisexual and so on. but in ancient society, it was not so because distant cultures had no conception of sexuality as an identity. Today when we talk about Islamic sexuality we think it is highly repressed in the past the early Islamics were nither homophobic nor sexually repressed as long as a man had sex with his own wives or slaves. In the 19th century, the westerners stigmatised the same-sex relationships in Islamic society this is when the Persian and Arab intellectuals began to put a halt on same-sex relationships.[150]

One of the dominant tropes of same-sex love in ancient India is through friendship, often leading to a life of celibacy or the forming of some very intimate

---

[149] Ibid

[150] Anna Clark, 'The History of Sexuality, We like to think of ourselves as having made progress from those repressed Victorians. However, since the 1970s, feminists, gay activists and historians have been questioning the notion of sexual repression. Anna Clark considers important recent studies on this most stimulating of subjects.' *HISTORY TODAY*, 9 September 2011. Retrieved from https://www.historytoday.com/archive/history-sexuality

relationships.[151] For instance, the friendship of Arjun and Krishna in the epic Mahabharata go beyond marriage and procreation. Krishna's affection for Arjun can be felt when he says Arjun is more important to him than any of his wives, kinsmen or children. He says there can be many wives but there can be only one Arjun. Same-sex desire is seen in ancient Bengali texts too, Kritivasa Ramayana (Ramayana written by Kritivasa) which talks about the birth of sage Bhagiratha who is born out of the union of two females.[152]

Fast forward to the 21st century, normative heterosexuality and marriage still remain the cultural norm. Heterosexuality dominates the porn industry. The relationship between porn and sexuality is very different for the LGBTQ+ community than for straight individuals. Lesbian sexuality has been repressed, rendered invisible, and impotent by society. The only way lesbian sexuality is represented in pornography that too for the pleasure of the male gaze.[153] The only way women are seen having sex is for the male imagination. In Victorian-era however close female friendships were celebrated, women could hug and kiss each other all night because it wasn't considered sexual. Recently the BBC film "The Secret Diaries of Miss Anne Lister '' shows, some of these women were having passionately sexual relationships.[154] Today's Pornography fails to portray

---

[151] Rohit K Dasgupta, University of the Arts London, 'Queer Sexuality: A Cultural Narrative of India's Historical Archive.', *rupkatha.com.* Retrieved from http://rupkatha.com/V3/n4/20_Queer_Sexuality_India.pdf

[152] Ibid

[153] Smyth, Cherry. âThe Pleasure Threshold: Looking at Lesbian Pornography on Film.â Feminist Review, no. 34, 1990, pp. 152â159. JSTOR, www.jstor.org/stable/1395314. Accessed 21 Aug. 2020. Retrieved from https://www.jstor.org/stable/1395314?seq=1

[154] Ibid. https://www.historytoday.com/archive/history-sexuality

women's pleasure, having represented it as a male construct with satisfaction only possible through penetrative sex.

Gay male pornography comprises of a large share of the pornography industry; it is estimated that 20-30% of pornography produced in gay male pornography, and this pornography creates 30-50% of the pornography industry's revenue.[155] Gay sexuality is less a problematic arena of pornography than lesbian sexuality due to the lack of gender power differentials. In other words, it is created by men for men Moreover, pornographic media displays are far from the reality of sex, and this leaves many gay men striving for something they may never reach.

Accurate queer community representation in mainstream pornography is mostly non-existent. Physical violence is not the only type of violence that exists against the heterosexual actor but it also exists in the queer community in the language used to categorize porn featuring gender-variant individuals. What's more? Many of the porn videos featured on top websites are made for men and are not really LGBTQA+ positive.

Several studies have found that gay men tend to experience greater body image dissatisfaction than straight men. Gay men have also reported greater social comparison pressures and pressures from the media, indicating that they may more susceptible to media influence on body image compared to straight men.[156]

---

[155] Neil Gleason, Minnesota State University, Mankato, 'The Effects of Pornography on Gay, Bisexual, and Queer Men's Body Image: An Experimental Study.', *Minnesota State University, Mankato*, 2017. Retrieved from https://cornerstone.lib.mnsu.edu/cgi/viewcontent.cgi?article=1710&context=etds

[156] Ibid

Pornography a Propoganda for Patriarchy

In the modern world, all women have the right to vote and as much as 47% of the labour force is made up of women, many people believe the battle for gender equality has been won but they couldn't be further than the truth because Over 2 billion women don't have the same employment options as men.[157] As we are evolving new issues are standing before us. The concept of equality requires equity.[158] According to UN Women "Equality does not mean that women and men will become the same but that women's and men's rights, responsibilities and opportunities will not depend on whether they are born male or female."[159] Leaders like B.R.Ambedkar,

---

[157] '10 Reasons Why Gender Equality is Important' *Human Rights Career.* Retrieved from https://www.humanrightscareers.com/issues/10-reasons-why-gender-equality-is-important/

[158] Ashima Obhan and Vrinda Patodia, 'India: Women Centric Changes In Indian Law', *mondaq,* 05 April 2019. Retrieved from https://www.mondaq.com/india/human-rights/795312/women-centric-changes-in-indian-law

[159] 'Concepts and definitions.', *UN WOMEN.* Retrieved from https://www.un.org/womenwatch/osagi/conceptsandefinitions.htm

Mahatma Gandhi, Raja Ram Mohan Roy and Savitribai Phule were in the forefront to encourage women to leave their families and homes where they were naturally confined to and bring them to schools, colleges and include them in independence movements. While the Indian judiciary has done away with triple talaq and amended the Maternity Benefit act the inequality that women face in society is still at large. In India, the constitutionally guaranteed equality is contradictory to societal norms.

The ugly traces of inequality can be seen right from school this can be understood through the detestable sexualisation of young girls, who are sent home from school for showing prepubescent knee caps and shoulders in their schools.[160] "look at what she's wearing," "doesn't she have any shame?" These are the types of comments we often hear from elderly people. What's more striking is. the lengths to which some young women will go to look "ideal women" putting their body and mind through agony and pain just to look perfect and fit in the eyes of societal norms.

This sexualisation issue is partly caused by the omnipresence of ideas relayed by mass media and porn. Could this be the reason why there is an increasing number of women who are going through a vaginal surgery even when many of them report that it has caused them physical discomfort and they

---

[160] Admin, 'A Fight For All: Why Feminism Is Still Necessary In The 21st Century', *INCITE*, 2018. Retrieved from http://incitejournal.com/opinion/a-fight-for-all-why-feminism-is-still-necessary-in-the-21st-century/

had to refrain from sex for at least 2-3 years?[161] While some women go through the surgery to please their spouse.[162] On the other hand, a study conducted on American women it was found that they go through cosmetic surgery because of body dissatisfaction, physical appearance, teasing (being teased about 11 different body parts) and media influence (feeling pressured to appear like people in the media).[163] They wish to alter their bodies because they despise their natural appearance, as it doesn't fit unrealistic expectations put forth by the media and wider society. This demonstrates how the objectification of girls is an all too real and undeniable issue, and in a world where women are asking for cosmetic vaginal surgery to feel prettier and worthier!

The sexual exploitation of women in pornography and the hypermediated nature of life in the contemporary World can undermine the ability of not only women but also men, who contribute in building the relationships which is stable, respectful to human communities and hence the sexual exploitation of women in porn the patriarchal mindset in

---

[161] Kashmira Gander, 'WHY WOMEN ARE GETTING COSMETIC SURGERY ON THEIR VAGINAS, The procedure costs thousands of pounds, but can improve the quality of life of some women', *INDEPENDENT* 24 November 2016. Retrieved from https://www.independent.co.uk/life-style/health-and-families/labiaplasty-why-women-are-getting-cosmetic-surgery-on-their-vaginas-a7436801.html

[162] Reviewed by Stephanie S. Gardner, MD 'Choosing Cosmetic Surgery', *WebMD*, February 03, 2019. Retrieved from https://www.webmd.com/beauty/choosing-cosmetic-surgery

[163] Furnham, Adrian, and James Levitas. "Factors that motivate people to undergo cosmetic surgery." The Canadian journal of plastic surgery = Journal canadien de chirurgie plastique vol. 20,4 (2012): e47-50. Retrieved from https://www.ncbi.nlm.nih.gov/pmc/articles/PMC3513261/

the society that we live in normalising it to such an extent that aggressive behaviour towards women is justified as being desirable or even sexy.

Pornographers and their allies have advanced their underlying libertarian sexual ethic, through giving porn a philanthropic twist, Pornhub started a bus tour called the "Boob Bus" which would go around the city creating awareness about breast cancer.[164] Ironically this is the same site which has various videos which show sexual abuses, studies have found that exposure to both violent and nonviolent porn increases aggressive behaviour, including both having violent fantasies and actually committing violent assaults.

Of course, consuming violent porn does not automatically make someone violent or abusive. Even so, the research has consistently shown in recent years how porn is inherently connected with sexual violence. It's worth considering just how much they're connected.

A recent research paper published in the Journal of medical internet research showed that consuming pornography increases the likelihood of physical and verbal sexual aggression.[165] The unfortunate thing is that this is not a completely shocking discovery since we have already seen the link between pornography and sexual violence, these findings only make the case more concrete. Science and research have shown how

---

[164] 'From Fashion To Adult Coloring Books, Pornhub Is Trying To Become America's Favorite Lifestyle Brand', *fightthenewdrug.org*, October 3, 2018. Retrieved from https://fightthenewdrug.org/ph-is-trying-to-become-a-lifestyle-brand/

[165] Carrotte ER, Davis AC, Lim MS Sexual Behaviors and Violence in Pornography: Systematic Review and Narrative Synthesis of Video Content Analyses J Med Internet Res 2020;22(5):e16702 URL: https://www.jmir.org/2020/5/e16702,DOI: 10.2196/16702,PMID: 32406863,PMCID: 7256746,

even non-violent porn consumers can be influenced by what they consume.

Here is a real-life story narrated by a Girl in Fightthenewdrug.com where she talks about her relationship turned abusive due to porn consumption:

"I was first exposed to porn at age 15 by my first boyfriend, and I had no idea the impact it would have on my life for the next six years. I didn't know what it was at that time but he told me that he'd watch it several times a day."

"Later in the relationship he wanted me to do extremely graphic scenes. If I refused, then he would watch porn, or harm himself."

"Towards the end of the relationship his obsession with porn became an all-time high, he was starting to get abusive he even assaulted me on several occasions"

"He finally left me when I developed PTSD, saying he couldn't handle me, I developed a habit to watch porn several times a week. It gave me a sort of comfort."[166]

Adult websites always try to mask their shortcomings and the ill effects it has on society. Websites like Pornhub have always done charity work like planting a tree for every 100 videos viewed from their "Big D—" category. Not long ago, "PornHub Cares," the "charity" department teamed up with porn performers for a campaign against domestic violence.

The campaign revolved around a particularly brutal case involving a couple of popular performers. In 2014 Christy Mack was brutally assaulted by her boyfriend UFC fighter Jon Koppenhaver a.k.a "War Machine". In August 2014 "War

---

[166] 'Porn Fueled Violence And Control In My Relationship—Here's How It Finally Ended', *fightthenewdrug.org* October 14, 2019. Retrieved from https://fightthenewdrug.org/true-story-violence-and-control-fueled-by-porn/

Machine" entered her apartment to find her sleeping alongside a male friend named Corey. He brutally attacked Corey and allowed him to leave on only one condition that he doesn't inform the police. After that, he physically assaulted Christy threateningly standing over her with a kitchen knife. He'd use the blade to slice off her long trademark Mohawk, she said. It was only when he left her alone that she went to the kitchen and grabbed a knife and escaped. This whole incident left her with 18 broken bones, shattered teeth and a ruptured kidney, among other injuries. She even had to visit a dentist for her broken teeth.[167] "I believed I was going to die," she wrote at the time. "He has beaten me many times before, but never this badly."[168]

During the 2017 trial after the violent assault, Christy testified that she and War Machine met on a set of an adult film and their relationship grew from that point. Mackinday told the courtroom that the relationship began to get abusive after "three or four months."[169]

---

[167] Nina Golgowski, 'Christy Mack opens up about relationship with MMA fighter War Machine, attack that left her near dead', *New York Daily News*, April 13, 2015. Retrieved from https://www.nydailynews.com/news/national/christy-mack-speaks-alleged-attack-mma-fighter-article-1.2183665

[168] Meera Jagannathan 'Christy Mack vs. War Machine: the whole ugly case, explained', *New York Daily News*, March 11, 2017. Retrieved from https://www.nydailynews.com/entertainment/gossip/christy-mack-war-machine-ugly-case-explained-article-1.2994559

[169] Russell Ess, 'Christy Mack in War Machine trial: 'He said now I have to take you into the desert and kill you', *BJPENN.COM*, March 10, 2017. Retrieved from https://www.bjpenn.com/mma-news/war-machine/christy-mack-in-war-machine-trial-he-said-now-i-have-to-take-you-into-the-desert-and-kill-you/

Although Mackinday was unable to fully recall the first abusive incident, she testified a few incidents that were vivid in her memory.

"He broke my phone in half, picked me up by my throat, brought me downstairs to my bedroom and threw me down,"

"He said now I have to take you into the desert and kill you," said Mackinday.

War Machine ended up being sentenced in 2017 to 36 years in prison for felony and misdemeanour charges stemming from the incident in 2014—involving kidnapping, sexual assault, attempted sexual assault, battery, and coercion, to name a few things—involving Mackinday and a male friend of hers while they were in her home.[170]

In response to this domestic violence case, pornhub partnered up with adult actress Christy Mack to create a new, "anti-domestic violence" clothing line the proceeds of which would go to charity.[171]

---

[170] 'The Disturbing Irony Behind Pornhub's "Anti-Domestic Violence" Campaign', fightthenewdrug.org, April 1, 2020. Retrieved from https://fightthenewdrug.org/site-launches-ironic-anti-domestic-violence-campaign/

[171] Dominique Sisley, 'Pornhub launches 'anti-domestic violence' clothing line, The site have partnered up with actress Christy Mack to help raise money for assault victims', *DAZED*, 21 January 2016. Retrieved from https://www.dazeddigital.com/artsandculture/article/29324/1/pornhub-launches-anti-domestic-violence-clothing-line

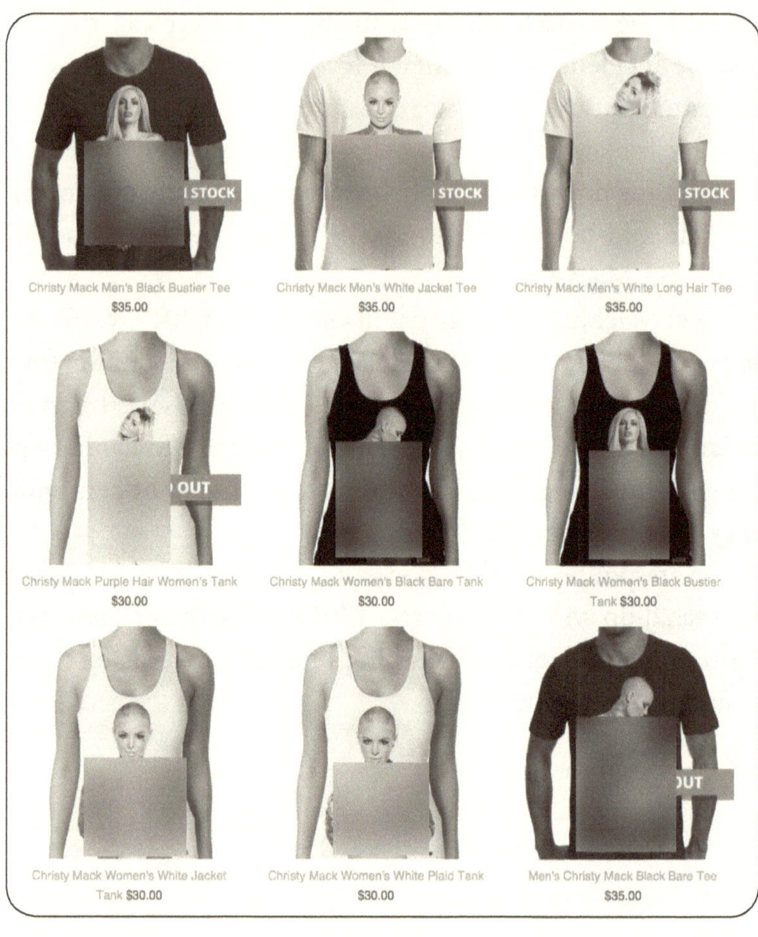

Website selling clothing line the proceeds of which would go to charity.
Image courtesy: FightTheNewDrug.com

Although it was a smart PR move for Pornhub to jump on an opportunity to give visibility to this serious issue, it's extremely hypocritical because their business involved Raising awareness on DV by day, selling abusive content by night.

Pornhub is one of the world's leading porn sites, which means that it is one of the world's leading promoters of fetishizing sexual abuse, including domestic violence.

These categories on the site like"wife abuse," "domestic discipline," "crying in pain," "extreme abuse," and "sleep assault."[172] acts as a form of sexual education, teaching the lesson that female sexual partners ought to enjoy these abuses.

One on hand pornhub capitalises off sexual abuse which is found all over their websites. on the hand, they do charity work which is apparently helping humanity fight domestic abuse.

Porn sites like cigarettes Brand back in the 50s and 60s have truly become experts on marketing sexual exploitation, further exploiting Mack by using her as a tool in their own agenda to appear concerned for domestic violence survivors, when in reality, they not only glamorize abuse but they also fuel it. Christy did not deserve any of what happened to her nor does any victim of domestic violence.

Another trend is taking place among the young generation is that of revenge pornography. This deals with non-consensual dissemination of intimate images.[173] Have you ever seen an awkward photo of yourself on social media, maybe it was posted by your friend who tagged you? You see the notification too late and now you had one or two comments saying how funny you looked. Now imagine that notification popping up except this time the photo is not embarrassing rather it's something sad and criminal. The sad part is everyone can see it too. This how the victim of revenge pornography feels. The aim of the culprit is to shame the victim using nude images. This is done with a view of vengeance and to wind up the relationship. Revenge porn can give the victim a post-traumatic

---

[172] Ibid. https://fightthenewdrug.org/site-launches-ironic-anti-domestic-violence-campaign/

[173] Aditya Krishnan, 'Revenge Pornography', *Legal Service India.* Retrieved from   http://www.legalserviceindia.com/legal/article-2179-revenge-pornography.html

stress disorder. The first case of Revenge porn could be back in the days when the adult magazine business was booming. Marilyn Monroe posed nude for a photographer named Tom Kelley in exchange for money. Things were going well for her until one day she saw her pictures in Playboy magazine. Being the first-ever issue Hugh Hefner sold around 50000 copies but Monroe had never signed a contract with him.[174] The craze for revenge porn grew with the rise of the internet. This is the new type of violence against both men and women which aims to threaten, shame and manipulate the victims is growing on the porn sites.[175] These videos can be taken down but by that time they are taken down the irreversible damage is already caused.

The glaring irony here is that the consumption of porn sexualizes the same violence many survivors endure. And in fact, in some instances, it can sometimes fuel it.

The journey towards equality and putting an end to patriarchy and the violence which stems from it is not a 'lone wolf challenge' but rather, the collection or coalition of the efforts of a committed group. By educating more people about porn we can control sexual and domestic violence.

---

[174] Ibid

[175] Written with assistance from Emily Hale, 'Three Ways Domestic Violence Is Connected to Pornography', *endsexualexploitation.org*, October 1, 2018. Retrieved from https://endsexualexploitation.org/articles/three-ways-domestic-violence-is-connected-to-pornography/

Pornstars and the Industry

The world's leading porn website gets 23 billion visits and is ever increasing. But who are the people working in this industry? The porn industry employs millions of people worldwide, mainly women. These range from the sex worker also called adult service provider (ASP) or adult sex provider, who provides sexual services, to a multitude of support personnel. Sex workers can be prostitutes, call girls, pornographic film actors, pornographic models, sex show performers, erotic dancers, striptease dancers, bikini baristas, telephone sex operators, cybersex operators, or amateur porn stars for online sex sessions and videos.

In recent years, porn has been accused of becoming increasingly violent. A veteran porn star said in a recent documentary about porn that, in the 1990s, it constituted "making love on a bed," and having "lovey-dovey sex". But in 2010, researchers analysed more than 300 porn scenes and found that 88% contained physical aggression. Sex was not always portrayed in this way, today BDSM is a leading genre in porn. When we talk about "BDSM" people often remember Fifty Shades of Grey which involves submission, sadism, or masochism although the practice may sound intimidating at first it was not the same case with Kamsutra. Vatsyayana talks about using teeth and nail-marks during coitus chapter IV Sutras 1-3 says when love becomes intense, scratching the body of one's lover with one's nails is practised. On the other hand, Kamasutra mentions teeth marks on different body parts. Vatsyayana also goes on to say that teeth should have the qualities of being even, shiny, of an attractive colouring, proportionate, close-set as well as pointed. It also gives importance to the consent of both parties.

In pornography, however, most persons who carry out a harmful act are male, and their targets female and the latter's most common response to aggression was to show pleasure or respond neutrally.

According to Business insider "a decade ago the average female performer would make about $100,000 a year," "but now they make as little as $50,000—all while juggling responsibilities such as social-media outreach and personal appearances. and this is from a report that's 5 years old, so in all likelihood, they're making even less than they were in 2012 because porn companies have unbundled more than ever."[176]

Once upon a time, porn used to be a lucrative industry. Most people could earn a steady source of income from adult magazines as well as the porn producers were considered no less than a celebrity. Popular porn stars would earn millions. But that's all changed, like almost everything else, since the internet became the major player in the porn industry. Now there are shrinking porn profits and a talent supply-and-demand imbalance which have caused performers' salaries to

---

[176] Aly Weisman, 'Here's What Female Porn Stars Get Paid For Different Types Of Scenes', *BUSINESS INSIDER* November 16, 2012. Retrieved from https://www.businessinsider.com/heres-what-female-porn-stars-get-paid-for-different-types-of-scenes-2012-11?IR=T

decline. This is because big companies like MindGeek, whose branches include PornHub, RedTube and YouPorn, and a dozen other brands have grown exponentially on the web these provide free porn since they profit from ads.[177] On the flip side, many tube sites rely heavily on pirated movies which means the studios don't get paid as they used to before when content was available only on VCR and DVDs, this also means that porn artists don't get paid enough. The traditional porn industry crash was also because more pirated content was available on the internet since 2008 through tube sites and torrents.

Since the porn business was going down MindGeek bought high-profile porn content producers, including big names like Digital Playground (in 2012), at discounted rates, each of them operating many sites.[178] MindGeek continued to purchase pirated videos too. This seems like a positive action to curb piracy, their model has been called a "vampire ecosystem" because the major profit pullers are MindGeek and producers don't earn as much.[179]

Since the porn industry workers do not have many options as the industry is dominated by MindGeek, the producers make films mostly for the sake of uploading it on the MindGeek's websites which earns lower returns for the producers and higher returns for the website. Actress Tasha Reign told ABC,

---

[177] 'What It Really Costs (And Pays) To Be A Porn Performer Today', *fightthenewdrug.org* May 29, 2020. Retrieved from https://fightthenewdrug.org/the-real-costs-of-performing-in-porn-today/

[178] David Auerbach 'Vampire Porn MindGeek is a cautionary tale of consolidating production and distribution in a single, monopolistic owner.', *SLATE,* October 23, 2014. Retrieved from https://slate.com/technology/2014/10/mindgeek-porn-monopoly-its-dominance-is-a-cautionary-tale-for-other-industries.html

[179] Ibid

"I kinda have to shoot for [MindGeek] because they own almost everything."[180]

Over the past few years, the porn industry claims that its very existence is threatened because of ever-increasing privacy. Studios have the remedy by taking legal actions against these websites, but that takes time and costs money, and ultimately isn't often worth the effort. performers are resorting to subscription-based models where they shoot their own scenes and sell but this works only for stars for newcomers they need to join the mainstream to make their name and earn money.

The performers are under more pressure to film more extreme acts even if it's painful because these types of scenes earn more profits. Steven Spielberg who represents top pornstars talks about how much the performers are paid according to him, $800 for a girl-girl scene, whereas for a standard scene it would be $1,000 which would involve guy-girl scene if the performers are willing to perform more extreme then $1,200 or more for anal sex and $4,000 or more for "double penetration"

Hence we can see how a performer could end up acting in more and more extreme scenes, even if they aren't comfortable doing it, and even if a chunk of their paycheck goes into paying medical bills as a result. the performers have to do harm if not dangerous acts just to make ends meet, a genre like torture porn earns a lot of profit but it's a sheer violation of Human Rights.[181]

---

[180] Andy Maxwell, 'Why Are Porn Perfomers Scared to Talk About Internet Piracy?', *torrentfreak.com,* April 13, 2014. Retrieved from https://torrentfreak.com/why-are-porn-perfomers-scared-to-talk-about-internet-piracy-140413/

[181] Ibid. *businessinsider.com* https://www.businessinsider.com/heres-what-female-porn-stars-get-paid-for-different-types-of-scenes-2012-11?IR=T

Increasingly, there's no such thing as a "regular" performer, there are those performers who do more extreme acts and stay in the industry and there are those who don't who get kicked out. This cycle feeds the demand for increasingly abusive and extreme scenes, creating a climate in which each scene needs to be more extreme than the last if it's going to be profitable for directors, studios, and performers. An AskReddit threat in July 2018 revealed some disturbing dirty secrets of the industry. "I experienced what was packaged as a 'rough sex' scene, I had bruising and tears and it was traumatising."[182] The same user also said her male actor in the film was too big for her, she was crying in pain but when the film was released the producer said that the consumers enjoyed the porn film.

Actors in porn are numb to life, being addicted to cocaine and meth they can't give up these addictions easily as it helps them to repress the brutal acts that they go through on the set. The consumers don't want to know that because it ruins their fantasy. Another porn performer by the name "R" reveals that she had to go through a surgery for catching a disease "After only thirty movies I caught two sexually transmitted diseases. "I got herpes, a non-curable disease and HPV. The HPV led to cervical cancer and I had to have half of my cervix removed. Porn destroyed my life."[183]

Saki Kozai, a young 24-year-old model thought her life was taking a turn for the better when a model scout spotted her on a Tokyo street and offered her job in promotion videos she later

---

[182] 'Porn stars share 'dirty secrets", *The OBSERVER*, 27th Jul 2018. Retrieved from https://www.gladstoneobserver.com.au/news/porn-stars-share-industry-dirty-secrets/3478689/

[183] Jorge Keek, 'The dark side of the adult film industry: Female porn stars speak out', *filmdaily.co*, 3 July 2020. Retrieved from https://filmdaily.co/news/female-porn-stars-abuse/

discovered that her job involved having sex on the camera. She said "There were 20 people around her and no woman can say no when they are surrounded like that"[184] Kozai got hooked on tranquilisers to deal with the anxiety the producers told her to cut off any contacts with her family so that she could focus more on her work, this had left her isolated. Most girls who enter porn at the age of 18 have no idea what contract they are signing. They usually last in the industry for 1 to 6 months 1 year at max when they realise that this is not something they'd subscribe to.

Lisa Ann, formerly the most researched pornstar on the web, performed for 20 years, unlike most performers who can only manage for six months to a year. While speaking to The Guardian she says there is a growing demand for hardcore porn and a lot of performers use drugs and have to do abusive scenes to meet the demand and this breaks them down as a woman.[185]

Building out a resume to include the more extreme stuff can be more lucrative, but once a performer says "yes" to doing an abusive or violent scene once, they've set the precedent for future scenes that set the bar into more and more extreme territory.

There have also been several reports out of the porn industry of performers who give their content to more Rough or Extreme acts but end up getting abused.

---

[184] Aseanplus News, 'Tricked into porn: Japanese actresses step out of the shadows', *TheStar*, 5 Oct 2016. Retrieved from https://www.thestar.com.my/news/regional/2016/10/05/tricked-into-porn/

[185] Dave Schilling, 'Lisa Ann: how one of porn's biggest stars transformed into a fantasy football guru', *The Guardian*, 26 January 2016. Retrieved from https://www.theguardian.com/culture/2016/jan/26/lisa-ann-porn-star-fantasy-football-sarah-palin

According to Rashida Jones, the producer and director of the Netflix documentary Hot Girls Wanted:

"The pay can be $800, $1,000 a shoot, but they still have to pay for hair and nails and makeup and travel and clothes—plus, they're trying to live lavishly, so it ends up not being cost-effective. It's not worth it. Then you have to make further negotiations with yourself, like, 'Will I do torture porn? Will I do fetish porn? Will I do…forced blowjobs?' and things that you never expected to do."

In another, not so shady and abusive world of adult explicit material world there exists Feminist and ethical porn where actors are paid and boundaries are respected. There's a lot of discourse in ethical and queer porn the real problem being that since this is a small industry as compared to mainstream porn the performers are paid less. The ethical porn industry does endeavour to make ethical porn at par with mainstream porn and possibly even surpass it. Ms. Naughty who found Mainstream porn to be "Sexist and Negative" was then inspired to start feminist porn. She says "It's an attempt to capture more realistic expressions of sexuality".[186]

There are Feminist Porn Awards organised every year where people get the opportunity to interact and devise a roadmap for the industry. filmmaker Tristan Taormino believes that "If you care about the conditions under which your food was made then, you should care about the conditions under which porn is made." "You should also be eager to pay a little extra

---

[186] 'Ethical porn does it exist and where do you find it', *abc.net*, December 20, 2016. Retrieved from https://www.abc.net.au/news/2016-12-21/ethical-porn-does-it-exist-and-where-do-you-find-it/8091266

for the industry to flourish"[187] The feminist porn conference also acknowledge that women work in this industry not because of choice but due to economic circumstances and sometimes even coercion. But even feminist porn is not devoid of criticisms. Anti-porn feminists and people opposing porn in general often believe that "Porn is turning us into voyeurs of others' lives, instead of masters of our own."[188] While some believe that feminist porn is a small niche market. RMIT researcher Meagan Tyler who has written a book on the ethics of commercial sex believes that "people who consume ethical porn like to believe that their consumption is unproblematic because they are consuming totally different from what others are consuming whereas in actuality they are fueling the same commercial sex industry".[189]

---

[187] Rachel Rabbit White, 'What Is Feminist Porn? "It's making a statement that women should be allowed to watch whatever kind of porn they want to watch," says porn star Courtney Trouble.', *buzzfeednews.com* May 2, 2013. Retrieved from https://www.buzzfeednews.com/article/rachelrabbitwhite/what-is-feminist-porn

[188] Liz Walker, '"Ethical Porn": A Smokescreen for an Exploitative Industry', *CULTURE REFRAMED,* February 17, 2019. Retrieved from https://www.culturereframed.org/ethical-porn-question/

[189] Ibid. *abc.net* https://www.abc.net.au/news/2016-12-21/ethical-porn-does-it-exist-and-where-do-you-find-it/8091266

Porn and Sexual Dysfunction

Does masturbation cause illness or problems in the body? the answer is No. Having a high sex drive also does not equate addiction. There is overwhelming scientific data available which says masturbation is healthy for men as well as women. Likewise, Masturbating also won't make you go blind, cause you to grow hair on the palms of your hands or any of the other "100% certain" side effects that you might have also heard about.[190] Masturbation helps you to figure out what turns you on sexually and what turns you on. Lots of people masturbate of all ages, and all genders even if they don't talk about it. Many people feel a deep self-hatred and shame for masturbating and this is because the societal norms that dictate "it is a dirty habit" or religious and cultural traditions sometimes associate self-pleasure and masturbation with feelings such as shame and sin.

Dr. Leena Mohadikar, a leading sexologist and writer from Pune writes in her book 'Kamaranga', "People have

---

[190] Written by Editorial Team & medically reviewed by Ho Anh, MD., 'Masturbation, Porn and ED: What You Need to Know', *hims,* 15 september 2017. Retrieved from https://www.forhims.com/blog/masturbation-porn-and-ed-what-you-need-to-know

a lot of misunderstandings about masturbation. These misunderstandings are magnified when society discusses misleading and false perceptions of masculinity and femininity, because of these wrong perceptions men and women start associating masturbation with weakness, fear, sin and shame."

When individuals associate shame with masturbation it is when the problem starts. Many times we use shame and guilt interchangeably but they are not the same.[191] At Least in this context both the words are different. Guilt acknowledges negative feelings over an action taken while shame tells you that because of a particular action you are not a worthy person. Shame makes you feel "You will never amount to anything", "I am unlovable", "I am defective" shame can make a person addicted to substances or in this case masturbation, one will feel shame when they masturbate and then to escape this feeling they masturbate compulsively. This is where Porn and masturbation can cause problems. As one gets more pleasure masturbating to porn they will develop a compulsive habit to watch porn and masturbating and this vicious cycle of shame and addiction continues.

Can too much masturbation cause erectile dysfunction? even though this is a common belief it's not true. but some peer-reviewed studies do show that too much porn can be related to sexual dysfunction.[192] Evidence is mounting that today's porn can not only be addictive but also impair sexual performance. This applies to erectile dysfunction (ED), delayed ejaculation

---

[191] Megan Bronson, 'THE DYNAMICS OF SHAME AND ADDICTION', *PHOENIX SOCIETY FOR BURN SURVIVORS*, August 27, 2019. Retrieved from http://www.phoenix-society.org/resources/breaking-free-of-the-addiction-shame-cycle

[192] Ibid. *hims,* https://www.forhims.com/blog/masturbation-porn-and-ed-what-you-need-to-know

(DE), premature ejaculation (PE), low libido and anorgasmia. Sexual dysfunction is no more an old man's disease because an increasing number of young men are having ED(erectile dysfunction) in the 21st century.

Over the last few decades, there's been a sharp rise in the incidence rate of sexual dysfunction – including erectile dysfunction, or ED – amongst men under 40.[193]

The rise has been difficult to explain through conventional means since today's population is in good health and faces fewer sexual restrictions than any other generation.

The cause, some researchers believe, could be the widespread availability of porn. Porn's ease of accessibility makes it a potentially serious cause of ED for young men.

Until recent years ED was extremely low among sexually active men. A study from 1999 revealed that the erectile dysfunction was at just 5% in men aged between 18 to 59, In 2002 the rate was merely 2%.[194] Then again in a study in 2011 on European men, the erectile dysfunction between 18-40 years was recorded at 14-28%. A year later, a Swiss study recorded a 30% ED in men aged 18-24 years.

In short, the rates of ED are seen more among young men, mainly among those who are in their 20s and 30s. In a 2014 study, the 11 out of 19 participants who used internet

---

[193] Park, Brian Y et al. "Is Internet Pornography Causing Sexual Dysfunctions? A Review with Clinical Reports." Behavioral sciences (Basel, Switzerland) vol. 6,3 17. 5 Aug. 2016, doi:10.3390/bs6030017. Retrieved from https://www.ncbi.nlm.nih.gov/pmc/articles/PMC50 39517/

[194] Laumann EO, Paik A, Rosen RC. Sexual dysfunction in the United States: prevalence and predictors [published correction appears in JAMA 1999 Apr 7;281(13):1174]. JAMA. 1999;281(6):537-544. doi:10.1001/jama.281.6.537. Retrieved from: https://pubmed.ncbi. nlm.nih.gov/10022110/

pornography reckoned that they "experienced diminished libido or erectile function specifically in physical relationships with women.[195]

Kinsey Institute was among the first one to research on pornography-induced erectile-dysfunction (PIED) and pornography-induced abnormally low libido, in 2007. Half of the subjects recruited were from bars and bathhouses, where video pornography was "omnipresent", in reactions to video porn these said subjects were unable to get an erection. researchers while talking to these subjects discovered that the high exposure to pornography resulted in low responsivity and an increased need for more extreme porn, specialized or even "kinky" material to have the same amount of arousal.[196] Over time this leads to a loss of libido and the notion of sex that is totally different from real-life relations.[197] The researchers redesigned their study so that by including more clips the subjects could choose from them. They came to the conclusion that a quarter of the participants' genitals still did not respond normally.

---

[195] Voon V, Mole TB, Banca P, et al. Neural correlates of sexual cue reactivity in individuals with and without compulsive sexual behaviours. PLoS One. 2014;9(7):e102419. Published 2014 Jul 11. doi:10.1371/journal.pone.0102419. Retrieved from: https://pubmed.ncbi.nlm.nih.gov/25013940/

[196] Ibid, https://www.ncbi.nlm.nih.gov/pmc/articles/PMC5039517/

[197] Urology professor Carlo Foresta, 'Too Much Internet Porn May Cause Impotence', *YOUR BRAIN ON PORN*, February, 2011. Retrieved from https://www.yourbrainonporn.com/porn-induced-sexual-dysfunctions/experts-who-recognize-porn-induced-sexual-dysfunctions-along-with-relevant-studies/too-much-internet-porn-may-cause-impotence-urology-professor-carlo-foresta-2011/

A clinical report published in Behavioural Sciences will help us understand more about how men are dependent on porn for artificial stimulation[198]:

A 20-year-old serviceman had difficulty in achieving orgasm during sexual intercourse. Although it first happened while he was deployed overseas, it continued. Whenever he was masturbating for about an hour he wouldn't get an orgasm, his penis would lose its vigour and go soft. Throughout his deployment his difficulty in maintaining an erection and attaining an orgasm continued. After his return he started having problems with his fiancee because he could not ejaculate during intercourse, he would get an erection but no orgasm. Before having ED issues this was not the case.

He endorsed masturbating frequently for "years", and once or twice almost daily for the past couple of years. Since he got access to high-speed internet he relied on pornographic material. Initially, he viewed softcore porn which did not have the actual intercourse itself and that helped him to orgasm. However, gradually he would open many windows on his browser and watch more graphic material to stimulate himself. When he was preparing for deployment he was worried about being away from intercourse with his partner so he bought himself a sex toy which was essentially a "fake vagina" Initially he would get an orgasm within minutes but as was the case with the porn he grew more difficult to reach an orgasm.

Since returning from deployment, he continued masturbating once or twice a day using the toy and internet pornography. Although physically and emotionally attracted to his fiancée, the patient reported that he preferred the device to have sex because he found it more stimulating. He

---

[198] Ibid, https://www.ncbi.nlm.nih.gov/pmc/articles/PMC5039517/

did not have any issues in the relationship other than ED his fiancee was getting the feeling that he wasn't interested in her at all.

The researchers explained to him that hardcore pornography coupled with sex toys had desensitized him. They suggested him to stop watching porn and using a sex toy. Although he did not completely quit his relationship did begin to improve with reduction in porn. He was more intimate and had orgasms too.

Sexual dysfunctions not only affect the consumers who are in their late 20s and 30s. In a survey by an NGO called Rescue found that 70% of students who were surveyed had watched porn from the age of 10. Due to early introduction and addiction to pornography more and more youngsters are having some form of sexual dysfunction.[199]

Viagra, a drug used to increase blood flow to the penis and treat ED was mainly used by older men in poor health.[200] But since 2008 there has been a rise in the number of cases with men under 40 having problems with their orgasms. Although this might be a boom for the drug industry this has brought to our notice the leading cause of ED.

Doctors are treating ED with viagra for teens as young as 19, saying it's just performance anxiety. When he should

---

[199] 'Survey: 70% of boys began watching porn at 10 years', *The Times of India,* 25 July 2015. Retrieved from https://timesofindia.indiatimes.com/city/coimbatore/Survey-70-of-boys-began-watching-porn-at-10-years/articleshow/48209402.cms

[200] Amy Fleming, 'Is porn making young men impotent? Up to a third of young men now experience erectile dysfunction. Some are turning to extreme measures such as penile implants – but is kicking their pornography habit the only solution?' *The Guardian,* 11 Mar 2019. Retrieved from https://www.theguardian.com/lifeandstyle/2019/mar/11/young-men-porn-induced-erectile-dysfunction

have been actually asking him about his sexual health and porn usage. The blue pilled physicians need to be sensitized on the topic too if we have to eradicate the problem from the grassroots.

Quitting Porn

Pornography is like any other drug. Just like a Morphine addict the way to make one stop consuming this substance is to simply get him off morphine this sounds easier said than done but with dedication and willpower, it is possible. People start watching porn not because they are broken, empty, or have an addictive personality. Porn is appealing because orgasms feel good and are the result of giving in to the most powerful drive on the planet; the need to procreate. It's basically impossible to get bored of the sexual variety. A man or a woman will choose a new sexual partner over food and water. Normally, they don't have that many options, but pornography creates the illusion of choice.

The movies Matrix Trilogy perfectly exemplifies accepting the new truth and letting go of the conditioning and false narrative which is so prevalent and accepted by society at large that it becomes normal. In the Movie, Morpheus who has attained wisdom and has become aware of the Matrix offers two pills to Neo. Morpheus offers Neo Red Pill and Blue Pill symbolising truth and lie. Neo takes the Red pill which represents truth and he embarks on a journey to understand how the Matrix manipulates people who are still plugged into the Matrix believing its lies and becoming increasingly dependent on it. If you have read this book till here it means who have essentially swallowed the Red Pill. You have begun the journey of coming into acceptance of a previously rejected truth.

I once read an article about the **Five Stages of Grief** and how they relate to accepting the truth, they are as follows:

1. **Denial – Still Plugged in the Matrix**

    "There is no way porn can be harmful! I like watching porn my friends enjoy it too! I find it liberating, it lets me vent out my frustration and grief"

2. **Anger – post-Red Pill**

    "This is absurd why should I accept the claims of this book? Quitting porn and actually finding meaningful relationships sounds like jumping through a lot of hoops!"

3. **Bargaining – trying to unplug from the Matrix**

    "Maybe quitting porn does have some benefits. But I feel if I watch it once in a week or so I should be good to go"

4. **Depression – Getting a bitter taste of Red Pill**

    "Great! Is that why I have been awkward around boys and each relationship fails miserably. I have wasted so much of my time watching Pornography while completely ignoring the real dynamics of sex. I feel unworthy" etc.

5. **Acceptance – Becoming aware of the false narrative of sex**

    "Holy shit! Maybe this is the way porn industries work. I should give up my understanding of sex learnt through porn but hey! What do you think about my kinks?"

The human mind has a surprisingly difficult time distinguishing between real and imagined events. Part of the reason pornography is addictive is why scary movies are scary.

If you have made it to this part of the book chances are you watch porn occasionally or so. Or maybe you have a friend or colleague who does or maybe you're a healthy individual who wants to read about the negative aspects of porn on the brain.

As a kid (even growing up) I was fascinated by George Lucas's Films the Star Wars Saga. The movie is based on the adventures of characters in "A long time ago in a galaxy far, far away", where space travel is possible and humans and aliens interact with each other. The movie is based on the Power of the Universe or spiritual power or "The Force" as the Movie suggests. According to starwars.com "the Force is a mysterious energy field created by life that binds the galaxy together." Harnessing the power of the Force gives the Jedi, the Sith, and others sensitive to this spiritual energy extraordinary abilities, such as levitating objects, tricking minds, and seeing things before they happen.[201] The movie focuses on Luke Skywalker's quest to become a Jedi and the Rebel alliance's struggle with the evil Darth Vader and Galactic Empire who has established a dictatorship over the galaxy. While the Force can grant users powerful abilities, it also directs their actions. And it has a will of its own, which both scholars and mystics have spent millennia seeking to understand.

The Jedi masters and knights would use this energy to fight evil and attain peace within themselves and in the universe. To harness this power was not easy; one needed unconditional dedication and fierce discipline. Once a person was a Jedi

---

[201] 'THE FORCE', *STAR WARS*. Retrieved from https://www.starwars.com/databank/the-force

Knight he/she was unstoppable having spiritual synchrony of body and mind.

Quitting porn works in similar ways as it opens the door to become a Jedi Knight it opens a whole new horizon wherein you can achieve your dreams easily. The human body is amazing. It has self-healing mechanisms but we need to create time and space for the body to heal. Quitting porn just does that, it gives your brain enough time to heal from the detrimental effects of porn, once that is done one easily gravitates towards positivity and goals. While watching Porn causes dysfunctional relationships, lack of energy and motivation, lowered libido, among other things. Quitting porn just has the opposite effect plus many more advantages for your body and mind porn consumes your time and your sexual attention, but do you think about how that doesn't leave you with energy for much else? A demanding porn habit can definitely drain your body of the mental and physical energy it needs to keep up with the daily hustle of life. We have always had porn and nudity which was represented in the form of art but these were not easily available to people but now with online porn, we have so much content that we can't live long enough to watch it. By taking small baby steps like turning off the monitor, you can focus on being productive and making a difference in your life and others.

Many people deep in their porn routine can often be too busy releasing their sex drive through porn, they're not going to have much interest in real sexual intimacy with a partner. Research shows that young people today are having less sex as compared to prior generations, of course, we can't blame solely on porn but it is one of the leading factors. We have already seen how they experienced a lack of drive or the inability to perform with their partner. Young people's access to pornography is affecting their ability to cultivate deeper connections with their partners day by day they are getting numb to real-life relationships research by Neuropsychiatrist Valerie Voon from Cambridge University found the brains of habitual porn users showed great similarity to the brains of alcoholics.[202] By quitting porn, one can give time for the brain to heal itself and reclaim their energy naturally and have meaningful connections.

People often watch porn for several reasons, It could be an escape when they are stressed and they want to find relief at the end of the day, finding it accidentally, peer pressure or when they become overwhelmed by the daily decisions of life. But by getting this distraction out of your way you can really focus on the things that really matter to you and be accountable to your goals.

The instant pleasurable experience that porn creates makes one want to watch porn even more resulting in the less desire for the activities that previously got you excited. Hanging out with friends, playing sports, making music, connecting with people on a personal and spiritual level all these things lack the "instant gratification" that porn gives the brain.

Oxytocin is known as the love hormone, oxytocin influences social behaviour because it plays a pivotal role in bonding two people.[203] This hormone is responsible for the attraction and it has relationship-enhancing effects which

---

[202] Luke Gilkerson, 'Brain Chemicals and Porn Addiction: Science Shows How Porn Harms Us', *CovenantEyes*, Feb 3, 2014. Retrieved from https://www.covenanteyes.com/2014/02/03/brain-chemicals-and-porn-addiction/

[203] Markus MacGill-Medically reviewed by Michael Weber, M.D., What is the link between love and oxytocin?', *MedicalNews Today*, September 4, 2017. Retrieved from https://www.medicalnewstoday.com/articles/275795

include trust, empathy, fidelity and positive communication.[204] Because the chemical is naturally released during sex, giving you relaxed psychological stability watching porn triggers the release of dopamine and oxytocin as well, tricking your brain and essentially bonding you to the sexual experience of porn. Once this happens over some time one can never feel the need to attract real love into their lives as they are already getting the sexual experience from a MacBook or smartphone screen. Infants go into a brain development stage but new research shows that adolescents who are undergoing puberty are also going into a similar development and with most development going on in the pleasure centre of the brain. This makes the teenage brain more sensitive to sex and bodily changes that they are going through.[205]

Addiction is never a healthy thing, regardless of what it is different timelines in history have tried to normalise addiction whether it is speed pills during World War II or cigarette companies trying to tell people that tobacco smoking does not cause cancer.[206] Porn can create a constant need for sexual material that needs to be fueled but is never truly satisfied. Pornography is categorically created to hook consumers by

---

204 Adrienne Santos-Longhurst-Medically reviewed by Virginia Pelley, 'Why Is Oxytocin Known as the 'Love Hormone'? And 11 Other FAQs' *healthline Parenthood.* August 30, 2018. Retrieved from https://www.healthline.com/health/love-hormone#TOC_TITLE_HDR_1

205 '50 Reasons To Ditch Porn Forever In 2020', *fightthenewdrug.org,* August 17, 2020. Retrieved from https://fightthenewdrug.org/40-reasons-you-should-quit-watching-porn-today/

206 Ryan Jaslow, 'Big tobacco kept cancer risk in cigarettes secret: Study', *CBS NEWS,* September 30, 2011. Retrieved from https://www.cbsnews.com/news/big-tobacco-kept-cancer-risk-in-cigarettes-secret-study/

adding strong visual and psychological cues.[207] This cycle can quickly grow into an addiction for the consumer, which inhibits their ability to function like a normal person in the company of people, especially the opposite sex, and can also lead to serious and harmful behaviours like soliciting sexually exploited people to act out what they've seen in porn. Porn consumers often have unrealistic expectations from their partners and when these expectations are not met they think that partner is not interested or aroused. People in pornography are selected based on their penis sizes and actors go through plastic surgery and its not necessary that these actors are having an orgasm while filming the porn because they do it to get paid. Not making porn a part of your life is a sure way to get rid of unrealistic expectations because if you go into a bedroom hoping your partner will perform like a pornstar in most cases, unfortunately, you will be let down. Porn depression and anxiety is a vicious cycle a person who has social anxiety and or depression finds comfort in porn and this in turn gives more isolation, loneliness and thus more social anxiety and depression. Eating healthy food has positive effects on the body and mind hence we don't let fast food industries to teach us about eating healthy then how can we let porn industries teach us what is healthy sex. We know that pornography and other addictions or compulsions are used as self-medicating tools which only lead to feeling worse than before. The momentary escape only leads to feeling lower than before. Porn is a negative influence in your life, and an easy way to start feeling happier and more free is giving it the boot.

---

207 Neil Farber, 'To View or Not to View? That Is the Question Good or bad? It's a matter of motivation and moderation', *Psychology Today*, June 17, 2015. Retrieved from https://www.psychologytoday.com/us/blog/the-blame-game/201506/view-or-not-view-is-the-question

As talked about earlier, porn can be the onset of several different anxiety problems. When consumers feel like they have to be watching porn or can't stop thinking about it, it creates serious anxiety. Not to mention, this anxiety can transfer over to the bedroom and contribute to porn-induced erectile dysfunction. Eating junk food every day makes one crave it even more because the craving is never really satisfied unhealthy food can take a toll on mental health similarly porn which is unrealistic sex can have a toll on mental health too. Quitting porn essentially means you rewire your brain and unlike before you don't need to find comfort in porn anymore to escape depression and anxiety it is putting an end to the vicious cycle and towards a healthier mental state.

Porn users often feel shame. quitting it will mean no porn fueled shame anymore. quitting will also curb unrealistic expectations of the body and this will promote more body positivity among individuals. An important thing to keep in mind while quitting any habit is that it doesn't happen magically--you don't wake up one day and porn habit is magically gone. Building a habit takes time as does quitting a habit. This will take time and dedication and the process will look different for each individual. It is high time that we start respecting individuals as sexual beings as adults as well as teens in school. Kids are taught how the sperm meets the zygote but never what leads to this process or how their bodies function. Being sexually misinformed is the new norm wherein adolescents are taught to deny and dismiss their sexual urges something that comes naturally this is why consumers watch porn in secrecy and the secrecy surrounding the consumer's habit can have huge negative effects on life and shame can quickly settle in. users may find watching things you find unacceptable, but can't seem to stop hence kids need to be taught sex education successfully and they need to be told how porn is different from real sex. When this feeling of shame and guilt starts to take its toll, this toxic shame keeps one trapped in the destructive cycle of porn.[208] Assuredly one will feel relieved when a user breaks the chains of this vicious cycle.

A NoFap movement is built on Reddit which is spreading every year. Fap is basically an internet vernacular for self-love or masturbation. This community aims to quit Porn and masturbation.[209] This online community on Reddit called NoFap found that 67% of those who quit porn and masturbation had an increase in energy levels as well as productivity.

Many people complain that they spend 20-30 hours on the weekend binging on porn, imagine this time could have been easily spent with friends, connecting with new people going on adventures.[210] there are stories of people being caught watching porn at work, this puts their jobs under threat. Porn induced lethargy is common when you masturbate to porn your mind is tricked into believing that you have impregnated multiple women that you seen, hence the life purpose of procreating and continuation of genes is complete. This is why people feel

---

[208] Luke Gibbons, 'How Toxic Shame Keeps You Trapped In The Destructive Cycle of Porn', *Conquer Series*. Retrieved from https://conquerseries.com/how-toxic-shame-keeps-you-trapped-in-the-cycle-of-porn/

[209] Dylan Love, 'Inside NoFap, The Reddit Community For People Who Want To Be 'Masters Of Their Domain', *Business Insider*, November 29, 2013. Retrieved from https://www.businessinsider.in/tech/Inside-NoFap-The-Reddit-Community-For-People-Who-Want-To-Be-Masters-Of-Their-Domain/articleshow/26554428.cms

[210] 'Help Me, I'm Wasting Time Looking at Pornography!', *forwardtherapy.com*, December 6, 2012. Retrieved from http://www.forwardtherapy.com/2012/12/help-me-im-wasting-time-looking-at-pornography/

a lack of motivation. Think about what is your purpose in life and what is stopping you from achieving it. Is it possible for you to be more motivated? Do you want to be more ambitious and driven? Are you wanting to achieve your goals?

The common belief is that pornography is for men and women who are single, who surf the internet a few days in a week browsing porn. Porn is for solidarity pass time is wrong notion people with who are in relationships view porn too, leaving us wondering if it affects them both. Relationships are hard work. They aren't always flawless, and sex won't be easy and perfect every single time. people who used pornography in a relationship say it helps them open up about sex, this can also provide an alternative outlet if their partner is not willing to have sex. In a study conducted Samuel Perry of the University of Oklahoma found that "while the majority of…studies generally assume that pornography use is causing marital problems, it could be that marital dissatisfaction leads to the greater use of pornography."[211] Real love in relationships can be messy but that's the beauty of it—it's real, not synthetic. porn has no way of showing this love because the focus is on the performance of different positions it is synthetic and not natural. The same study also found that men and women who viewed pornography in their relationships were more likely to be unhappy. Suggesting someone view pornography just because their partner is into it is not a good option either because this is not the case of "If you can't beat them, join them." Unrealistic expectations of porn can be detrimental

---

[211] Robert P. Burriss,'How Pornography Really Affects Relationships New studies of men and women find complex effects, and it's not all bad', *Psychology Today*, October 25, 2016. Retrieved from https://www.psychologytoday.com/intl/blog/attraction-evolved/201610/how-pornography-really-affects-relationships

to a relationship which goes on to normalise abuse.[212] Real intimacy with your partner on the other hand offers so much more it does not involve abuse verbal or physical. Many men have reported that they need to think about porn to get an erection when they are with their partner.

People are also found to be using porn when their relationships don't go well. But this can cause havoc in relationships when porn use goes out of hand rather they should talk it out or seek professional help. Real intimacy is indeed a world of satisfaction and excitement which doesn't disappear when the smartphone screen goes off. Porn doesn't portray true connections, real intimacy is being vulnerable to your partner taking risks and building bonds. Real men and women have flawed bodies unlike pornstars and being intimate in relationships also means exploring thoughts and feelings, something that the screen does not offer.

A study also found that couples who watched porn were twice more likely to get divorced.[213] This isn't surprising because when porn has clouded a consumer's idea of what healthy marriages are.

Getting porn out of the picture means that you're one step closer to healing from the lies that porn infects consumers

---

[212] Marni Feuerman-Medically reviewed by Carly Snyder, MD. 'Is Pornography Destroying Your Marriage?' *verywellmind*, January 28, 2020. Retrieved from https://www.verywellmind.com/is-pornography-destroying-your-marriage-2302509

[213] Shankar Vedantam, 'Researchers Explore Pornography's Effect On Long-Term Relationships', *npr*, October 9, 2017. Retrieved from https://www.npr.org/2017/10/09/556606108/research-explores-the-effect-pornography-has-on-long-term-relationships#:~:text=Researchers%20Explore%20Pornography's%20Effect%20On%20Long%2DTerm-%20Relationships%20Married%20men,worse%2C%20increasing%20the%20divorce%20risk.

with. The key to a long-lasting strong relationship is the couples ability to build strong emotional intimacy.[214] In the real world having this takes a lot of time, many times things don't go as planned but in long term, this always has positive effects when the relationship does work out. In porn, however, there is quick satisfaction with dopamine release but in the long term as we know the effects are bad.

[214] Gary Gilles, 'How Pornography Distorts Intimate Relationships', *MentalHelp.net*. Retrieved from https://www.mentalhelp.net/blogs/ how-pornography-distorts-intimate-relationships/

Epilogue

Pornography is only one google search away and is becoming ever more immersive. Pornography has gone through a dramatic change in the last 50 years. From nude images and erotic stories in novels and magazines to sex toys and virtual reality. Pornography is not inherently problematic, rather how some people are represented in pornography are is the real problem.

According to Covenant eyes which provides statistical research: there are 90% of teens and 96% of young adults who are either encouraging, accepting, or neutral when they talk about porn with their friends. the 21st century is going through a change concerning how we look at sex and sexuality.

Extensive scientific research reveals that exposure to and consumption of porn threatens the social, emotional and physical health of individuals, families and communities, and highlights the degree to which porn is a public health crisis rather than a private matter. Since sex ed is not a topic discussed in schools and in our society moreover it is looked down upon and even dismissed. According to Sigmund Freud, the father of psychology, sexual repression was the chief psychological problem ailing mankind. He said that constriction and repression of sexual behaviour in youth would manifest in adulthood. whenever an attempt is made to understand sex a scientific knowledge is not available moreover the societal norms consider sex as taboo and frown upon ways to relieve one's sexual urges, especially if practised by the unmarried this leads sexual repression and perversion of sex. In the online survey that we conducted, 41% of individuals first came to know about sex from friends, 20% from movies and 17% from Porn.

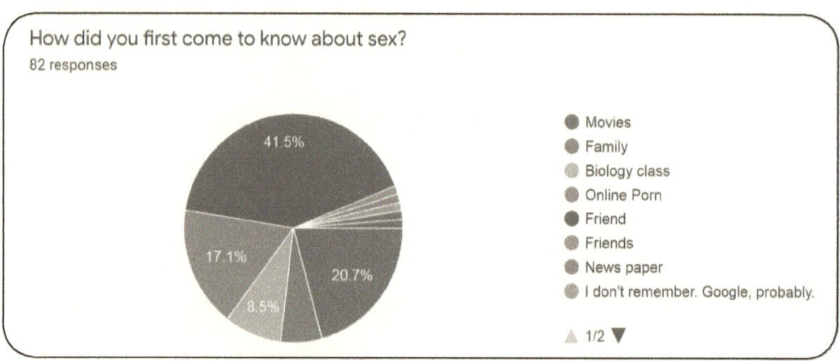

Among adolescents, there is a natural sexual impulse but people are either dismissive or simply shy away from the topic, the curiosity and pleasure lead people to consume more and more of this porn as understanding sex through scientific temper are not readily available as compared to Porn. The Porn industry on the other hand has taken full advantage of this sexual perversion and lack of knowledge. Those who protest against these industries are deemed anti-sex instead of anti-violence.

These industries feed on people's lack of understanding. If we are more sensitized about sex then the number of porn consumers would naturally decrease. An educated audience for porn would mean they will have to regulate porn and stop normalising abuse, this would also mean porn would be completely off-limits to those who are under the age of 18 and when adolescents are taught about sex and their body in a positive pragmatic way their understanding about sex would be different from now and they wouldn't feel the need to seek sexual pleasure from a screen which shows exploitative sex.

Testimonials

"...Human beings trapped in pleasures of mind and body; seek escape through religion, meditation, sex, alcohol, drugs and whatnot. Sex is elevated to divinity as in Shiva and Shakti Cults. While sex is sublime, porn is an aberration. Fortunately, their shelf life is short, unlike other lifelong vices. Prasenjeet Dhage, standing on the threshold of adulthood has made a bold attempt to explore the role played by the hormone dopamine on sex, porn, alcohol and drug abuse..."

– Ramakant Khalap, Writer, Ex Dy.Chief Minister of Goa and former Union Law Minister of India.

* * *

"...I congratulate a law college student for undertaking a daunting task of writing such a book titled ''The Dopamine Trap: Sexuality and Pornography in 21st century›. The future generation may doubt, like "Dnyaneswari", how a budding in unmarried boy could write such a book in the orthodox rotten culture dominated by the Hegemony of a single priestly Americanized Eurocentric caste. Since I have completed three

Volumes on Cultural Studies I understand the significance of such sincerity and courage…"

– Dr. Anand Patil, Creative writer and Critique.

"…This is a spine-chilling book, Prasenjeet Dhage has so far made his advocacy work dynamic to convey the key message of his book, Dopamine Trap. What I love most is how Prasen draws on consequences, effects, and other aspects of life to help readers let go of regrets, relive the past, and pursue their life dreams…"

– Her Excellency, Helen Mukoro Idisi, Spanish politician. First black presidential candidate in Spain and Europe.

www.ingramcontent.com/pod-product-compliance
Lightning Source LLC
Chambersburg PA
CBHW051052250726
48656CB00001B/268